THE
HERBERT J.
TAYLOR
STORY

InterVarsity Press
Downers Grove
Illinois 60515

All Scripture quotations not otherwise identified are from the King James Version of the Bible.

The Four-Way Test *and* The Ten Marks of a Good Citizen *referred to in this book*
are © *1946 by Rotary International.* The Twelve Marks of a True Christian
is © *1964 by H. J. T.*

InterVarsity Press is the book-publishing division of Inter-Varsity Christian Fellowship,
a student movement active on campus at hundreds of universities, colleges and
schools of nursing. For information about local and regional activities,
write IVCF, 233 Langdon St., Madison, WI 53703.

Distributed in Canada through InterVarsity Press, 860 Denison St., Unit 3,
Markham, Ontario L3R 4H1, Canada.

ISBN 0-87784-836-X

Library of Congress Catalog Card Number: 68-28440

Printed in the United States of America

15	14	13	12	11	10	9	8	7	6	5	4	3	2	1
94	93	92	91	90	89	88	87	86	85	84	83			

*This book is dedicated to the youth
closest to my heart—my grandchildren—
Caryl, Gayle and Allen Mathis, and Becky,
Jeffrey, Sally and Greg Lockhart.*
Herbert J. Taylor

Table of Contents

Publisher's Preface

Herbert J. Taylor (1893-1978) was a remarkable man. Energetic, success-oriented, inventive, practical and indefatigable, yet honest, sensitive, compassionate, loving and deeply religious. His story is worth telling and retelling as an inspiration to others and as a record of what can happen when a person is wholeheartedly devoted to doing the will of God.

Testimonies abound to the impact Herbert Taylor made on the lives of leaders around the world. His long association with Rotary brought him in contact with a large number and wide variety of business people. He served as president of the Chicago Rotary Club (1939-40) and Rotary International (1955). One recent past president of Rotary International (1975-76), Ernesto Imbassahy de Mello, summed up his contribution this way:

> For him, thought and action were a couple. In his pragmatism he used to say: Get the facts; develop a plan; follow through. He was genuine and congruous in thinking, saying and doing. Herbert J. Taylor: a devoted man of faith, an outstanding citizen, and a remarkable Rotarian. His name is inscribed in the story of Rotary, for he wrote part of it.

Stanley E. McCaffrey, another past president of Rotary International (1981-82), agrees:

Herb Taylor was a unique combination of an idealist, being a dedicated Christian, and at the same time a very practical person. It was out of this combination of the idealist and the practical man that he developed The 4 Way Test which has made such a positive contribution in helping resolve difficult situations in hundreds of thousands of instances throughout the world.

Perhaps Herbert Taylor will be remembered the longest for his contribution to the founding and support of many Christian organizations, especially those with a ministry to high-school and college students. Much of that story Herb Taylor tells here in his own words. The impact of his faithfulness to God's work can best be expressed by those who experienced it. Hear the words of Sam Wolgemuth, president emeritus of Youth for Christ International:

God spoke to us through Herb Taylor. His "can-do" spirit was infectious. Herb wanted action. A man of vision, he had faith because he had seen God at work in other organizations.

Herb had proven his personal discipline and earned his integrity in the tough, competitive business world. That gave him a platform others listened to, and Herb used that platform to express his deep love for young people.

His love for the Word and a dedication to the will of God made his life a continuing miracle. As a result, the Lord gave him a powerful role in changing lives and affecting the destiny of souls.

Herb Taylor's influence, perception and gifts played a strategic role in the ongoing development of Youth for Christ worldwide. We will always be grateful.

Billy Graham echoes these sentiments:

Herb Taylor was one of my closest friends and confidants for nearly thirty years. He was a constant source of encouragement. He set an example in his personal life that made an indelible impression on me.

The memory of Herbert Taylor lingers in my heart and mind. His being in heaven makes heaven closer.

Lorne Sanney, president of the Navigators, was also influenced by Herb Taylor:

Mr. Taylor was a treasured personal friend who walked with God and generously shared with us from his wealth of wisdom and experience. The Navigators greatly benefited from his membership on our board and from his godly counsel. His influence will long be remembered.

And James McLeish, president of Inter-Varsity Christian Fellowship, comments:

Herb Taylor was a leader who had the vision and the tough-mindedness needed to get the job done. That drive helped start Inter-Varsity Christian Fellowship in the U.S.A., helping thousands of students hear the gospel and grow in the faith. His memorization of large portions of Scripture gave him wisdom and made him a great man of God.

Herbert Taylor had a profound effect on those who worked closely with him. Ken Hansen, one of the incorporators of ServiceMaster, a former president and former chairman of ServiceMaster Industries, Inc., whom Taylor mentions on page 78, says, "Herb's sayings have stuck in my mind and molded my life." Hansen refers specifically to The 4 Way Test, RMA (right mental attitude) and FE (fighting enthusiasm). Keith Hunt, director of Cedar Campus, which Taylor often refers to in his story, points to Taylor's "consistent source of help and encouragement. His positive 'can-do' attitude was demonstrated to me time and again to encourage me to believe God for things which seemed impossible."

Hunt recalls an incident at Cedar Campus that captures Taylor's joy in life:

Mr. Taylor's eyes always had a look of deep pleasure and enjoyment when he was at Cedar Campus. He had come to this spot as a boy with his own father, and he never failed to appreciate what a special setting it was. One time when his grandson Greg Lockhart was fishing on the dock, he caught a good-sized smallmouth bass. He was so excited he wanted to run back to the cabin to show his mother and father. He gave his fishing pole to his grandfather to hold while he went back to show off his prize. Mr. Taylor sat on the edge of the dock, talking to us, and suddenly he felt a pull on his fishing line, and said, "I do believe I've got a fish on here," and pulled up another good-sized bass. He was delighted! He wouldn't have taken time to go fishing—that wasn't his thing—but to have caught one by "accident" made him as happy as if he were a small boy himself.

As Robert Walker, president of Christian Life Publications, pointed out in his preface to the original edition of this book, Herbert Taylor tells only part of his own story. Taylor always focused on the positive aspects of life. But his own experience included "many disappointments, heartaches—even failures —that marred his path to success." What we don't see here are comments on an illness whose debilitating results lingered through the years. Sometimes while he was working and presiding over meetings, he was plagued with headaches. But as Walker says, "Still, no one suspected from his outward appearance that anything was wrong.... On the rare occasions that he has alluded to his physical infirmities, he has quoted his favorite New Testament author, Paul, in his classic statement of the Lord's overriding provision for whatever our needs may be in times of trouble: '... My grace is sufficient for thee: my strength is made perfect in weakness. Most gladly therefore will I rather glory in my infirmities that the power of Christ may rest upon me' (2 Corinthians 12:9)."

In 1975 Herbert Taylor suffered a debilitating stroke which drastically impaired his ability to speak, read and write. Kenneth Hansen writes of his visit with Taylor:

Herb drew me into the music-sitting room to the left of the foyer. Seating me next to himself on a small settee, he put his much-used Bible on his lap and then turned to the front fly leaf where he had listed the many long passages he had memorized and kept alive by repetition and application to life through the years. Then he pointed to each one—one at a time—and with face aglow and eyes sparkling, he'd say for each one, "Wonderful, Ken, wonderful!" and jab my knee with his forefinger and second finger in his typical old-time two-finger jab to make a point stick or to be sure I got the point. And, so we went through the list unhurriedly, savoring each passage of God's Word of truth. "Wonderful, Ken, wonderful!" Jab, jab! Talk about right mental attitude and fighting enthusiasm and the right balance, perspective and focus!

He was—and the memory of him still is—one of God's very special gifts to me.

We are pleased as the publisher to present this book which, as Kenneth Hansen says, "should not go out of print."

Since the first publication of this book in 1968, the organizations Herbert Taylor helped have grown and increased in their influence. Updated statistics will be found on page 129.

The Publisher
1983

Foreword

During my college days, while taking a leisurely walk with my father, he looked at me and said earnestly, "You know, Beverly, there are two kinds of people in this world, those who are led by the Holy Spirit and those who are not." Although I knew he was encouraging me to pray to God for an answer to a particular problem I had shared with him, I didn't fully understand what he was saying. Yet, somehow I couldn't forget those words.

It was some years later that I read in the Bible, "For as many as are led by the Spirit of God, they are the sons of God" (Romans 8:14). Then I realized that if I wanted the assurance of God's love and his guidance, I had to trust him with my all. After this commitment, I wondered why I had been so fearful, for now I was experiencing a bright new love, joy, purpose and hope in life.

In January of 1975 my father suffered a stroke on his right side that caused him to lose most of his reading, writing and speaking ability. His doctor diagnosed his condition as aphasia resulting from a stroke. Such an inability to communicate frequently leads to depression, withdrawal and irritability. Fortunately, Dad did not react in this manner. Instead he radiated a peaceful and even joyful countenance. To our delight he approached each day enthusiastically, even disciplining himself with speech and reading therapy, daily walks and devotions when he would listen to recordings of the Scriptures. His trust in the Lord seemed even more obvious in this trial. Once I said to him on his return from a walk, "Daddy, Jesus speaks to you, doesn't he?" and he nodded knowingly! This Bible verse came to my mind: "The Spirit itself beareth witness with our spirit, that we are the children of God" (Romans 8:16). It was quickly followed by the verse, "Commit thy works unto the LORD, and thy thoughts shall be established" (Proverbs 16:3).

Many years before Dad's stroke I had asked him why he memorized so much Scripture, some twenty-four chapters of the Bible, which he said over every day in his mind. He turned to John 14:21, where Jesus says, "He that hath my commandments, and keepeth them, he it is that loveth me: and he that loveth me shall be loved of my Father, and I will love him, and will manifest myself to him."

I believe God richly prepared my father for these last three and a half years of his life—years when he lived with so few of his former talents in speaking, reading and writing. How gracious of God to keep him so aware of his presence through the Word and the Holy Spirit in his heart.

My father believed in the importance of acting on what the Lord told him to do—not just the intellectual learning of many Bible verses. He made it a practice to use The 4 Way Test as a measuring stick to help him examine himself before the Lord.

It was my father's urgent desire that all, especially young people, hear early in life that God has a plan for them. Many times my sister and I heard him say, "Faith cometh by hearing, and hearing by the word of God" (Romans 10:17). He also quoted Jesus' words in John 10:10: "I am come that they might have life, and that they might have it more abundantly." Two other verses enlightened me. They are Jeremiah 29:11: "For I know the plans I have for you, says the Lord. They are plans for good and not for evil, to give you a future and a hope"

(TLB) and Psalm 37:5: "Commit everything you do to the Lord. Trust him to help you do it and he will" (TLB).

On May 1, 1978, my father's spirit went to a heavenly home. He was eighty-five and had lived most of those years in the joyful service of Jesus Christ. His favorite Bible verse has become increasingly precious to me: "Trust in the LORD with all thine heart; and lean not unto thine own understanding. In all thy ways acknowledge him, and he shall direct thy paths" (Proverbs 3:5-6).

Beverly Taylor Mathis

1

The Plan

ALMOST EVERY speaker knows that the most frightening and unpredictable audience he can face is one composed of intelligent, inquisitive teen-agers. It has been said by at least one businessman—a businessman who apparently knew little else, except business—that dealing face-to-face with an executive for a million-dollar deal, and coming away with the order, is the truest and hardest test of good salesmanship. I challenge him to attempt to change the mind of an alert teen-ager! To do so, he has to be a very well-rounded man, indeed,—familiar with philosophy, business, the good and bad of life and many other subjects. In addition, he has to have a good helping of faith, compassion, understanding and common sense.

So, it was not without some trepidation that I appeared before a large group of teen-agers at what is now known as Cedar Campus in the summer of 1948. That I had played a large part in building and developing this conference ground to train Christian leaders made little impression on my audience, nor did the fact that I was known to have helped develop and finance many other Christian organizations. That I was known as a successful businessman—well, that meant less than nothing. I was just Herbert J. Taylor, and I was going to say a few words to the audience. They would sit, and they would listen respectfully,

19

because I deserved that much. But—would I have anything help-ful to say to them?

Cedar Campus in on Prentiss Bay in northern Michigan—a resort area that used to have a great deal of logging activity. The logs were felled along the shores of the bay—or transported to the bay—then they were floated or poled to a local sawmill. As I learned from some of the lumbermen in the Prentiss Bay area, some of the logs made it and some didn't. Some floated well and went on to become useful and productive, while others slipped to the bottom of the lake almost as soon as they hit the water. These were known as deadhead logs and were quite visible be-neath the clear waters of Prentiss Bay.

I knew that everyone in the audience had seen those dead-heads, and, when I gave my talk before these young people, I based it entirely upon that fact. In effect, I said that there are two kinds of people, just as there are two kinds of logs. There wasn't a boy or girl in that audience who didn't immediately understand exactly what I was driving at. No young person wants to lead a dull, unproductive, deadhead life. They realized I understood that, and from that moment on I had an attentive, re-sponsive audience.

I want to start this book by saying that my most important consideration in writing this book is to say things that are perti-nent to *you*. Over the years, I've found answers to problems common to all of us, be we teen-agers, or adult men or women. I want to pass these answers along to you. I believe, deeply, that God has given me the privilege of writing to you, and that means I'm going to have His help in telling you about some experiences I've had over my more than seventy-year lifespan. These experiences can open doors to a wonderful and productive life for you—just as they have for me. If this is what you want—a truly meaningful and satisfying life—then we understand each other and, without further prelude, I'll start my story.

The third child of Frank and Nellie Taylor, I was born in Pickford, Michigan in 1893. A long time ago—another century

—but people and problems weren't nearly as different from ours as you may think. My developing years included a world war, foreign travel, the great depression of the thirties, a wide variety of jobs and extensive travel throughout the United States. In short, God granted me the privilege of knowing, living with and working with many kinds of people, in many kinds of places, under economic and social conditions that ranged from all-out war to the pride-destroying chaos of the decade, in which close to 30 percent of the people in this country couldn't feed their families a decent meal. No sensitive man lives through such wide-ranging experiences without learning a great deal about humanity: the needs, desires and, above all, the particular purposes of men that make life worthwhile—that replace frustration and doubt with certain victory. Just learning about these things and reflecting on them, however, is never enough, because unless knowledge and understanding are channeled in accord with a definite plan, the end result is often a confused muddle. In other words, nothing much is accomplished by understanding what it's like to be hungry, and then sympathizing with a hungry man. If you *feed* that man and relieve his hunger, your understanding becomes meaningful. I was blessed to have the experiences I did. They gave me insight into many human needs and problems. I was even more blessed to have been given a plan, early in my life, that enabled me to do something about the conditions I encountered.

When the United States entered World War I actively, I was already in France, serving with the YMCA. Shortly thereafter I enlisted in the U.S. Naval Reserve and was later commissioned a Lieutenant (jg). I was assigned to the U.S. Naval Base in Brest, France, and was placed in charge of the distribution of food and clothing for our Naval forces in French waters. At the close of hostilities, I was given a short leave of absence from the Navy in order to become Regional Director for the YMCA, in the Brest area. On their way to home-bound ships, 150,000 to 200,000 troops continually passed through this area. It was the YMCA's

21

job—and mine—to keep the boys occupied and provide them with facilities for entertainment, relaxation and worship. I was twenty-five years old at the time, and later often said, "After that job nothing ever appeared too big or too difficult."

During this period, I met several people who were to be instrumental in the formulation of the plan that I have followed all of my life—and which is the real subject and object of this book. George Perkins was in charge of raising funds for the YMCA's operations in France. Senator Robert L. Owen from Oklahoma knew about my administrative success with the Navy and the YMCA, and he suggested that I get in touch with him in Washington after my discharge. He said he could arrange a job appointment with Harry Sinclair, then President of the Sinclair Oil Company.

I did as he suggested and was offered a job with Sinclair. But I was also offered another—more tempting position—as assistant to the Associate General Secretary of the YMCA. I have always been keenly interested in young people and have always believed that the YMCA would play an ever-increasing role in the Lord's work, so this last job offer was mighty tempting. I felt, however, that I had God-given talent in administration and that my field might, more properly, be in business. I prayed about the situation and was clearly led to talk with George Perkins—(a partner in the New York financial house of J. P. Morgan).

I remember the afternoon vividly. I told Mr. Perkins my story; Mr. Perkins heard me out. Then he said, "You think I'm going to tell you to go with the YMCA, don't you? That is because you love young people—it's probably your first love, as compared to business. Well, that's not what I'm going to tell you. I suggest you go into business."

I was somewhat surprised by Mr. Perkins's statement, but he followed it up with reasons quickly.

"You have a considerable amount of God-given business talent," he said, "and I want to give you some advice. First, I think you'll be a success with Sinclair. Second, use all of your extra time to work with youth. As time goes by, I believe you'll be successful enough in business to have your own company, where you can influence the making of policies. You'll be able to take time away from business for your youth activities. By the time you're forty-five," he continued, "you'll be spending more of your time on young people's projects than on your business. In the last few years of your life, I believe you'll be working full time at it."

Everything Mr. Perkins said worked out, except that I didn't stay with Sinclair. I became successful in business and devoted my spare time to youth projects; I gained control of a company, influenced the setting of policies and, thereby, was able to devote even more time to young people. By the time I was about forty-five, the pendulum had swung. I was spending more time on the Lord's work than on business. In the last twenty years or so, I have been doing that most of my time. Mr. Perkins was the vehicle through which I'm certain God presented me with a plan —His particular plan for me. No man could have predicted my life with such accuracy, and surely no one but the Lord could have assured my survival to carry out the plan. From the moment I left Mr. Perkins' office, I knew the course of my life. It was one of the most confident and wonderful moments in my life.

Just to know *what* you are doing and *where* you are going is a tremendous blessing for a young man or woman. There isn't anyone on this planet who, if he will seek his *own* plan from God—sincerely, patiently, and with prayer, through Christ Jesus our Lord—won't have the facts revealed to him sooner or later, in one manner or another. The Bible says: ". . . to do those good deeds which God planned us to do" (Ephesians, 2:10, PHILLIPS).

Just wishing, however, is never enough. From the beginning —with God's plan for my life revealed and clearly in focus—I set about the task of doing what I could do best: following a career as a businessman, while setting aside time for that which, next to my own family, I loved most. I worked with young people continually and with God's help and direction; attempted to show them, by example, how productive and meaningful a young person's life can be if he will give himself over to God—to seek diligently for God's will for him and to follow it consistently.

2

I Learn the Ground Rules

PICKFORD, MICHIGAN, is in what is known as the Upper Peninsula. When I was born, I believe the town boasted about three hundred people. My father was active in several businesses in Pickford—lumber, banking, and the local telephone company. He and his brothers owned almost every business in Pickford! Uncle Fred ran the hardware store; Uncle Ed the grocery; Uncle Andrew the shoe store; Uncle George the dry-goods store.

My parents were devout Christians. I believe that the greatest blessing anyone can have is to have a fine Christian mother. The next greatest blessing is to have a fine Christian wife, children and grandchildren—in that order. Through the years God has surely given me all of these great blessings.

I can't say that I was too interested in religion during my early years. I went to Sunday school, but not as often as my parents wanted me to. Not until I was seventeen did I accept the Lord Jesus Christ as my personal Saviour. In those days, our little Methodist Church arranged for visiting evangelists to preach for a week or two each year, and I believe it was at the last meeting that I became convinced, stepped forward and accepted Jesus Christ as my personal Saviour and Lord. I don't mean to record that moment casually, but it was just that simple and straightforward. It was, and is, surely the most important event in my life.

My mother gave me my first Bible after that experience. Later I memorized two or three passages that began to have a profound influence on my thinking and my life immediately. The first passage is the 24th Psalm, first verse: "The earth is the Lord's, and the fulness thereof; the world, and they that dwell therein." That being true, then there wasn't anyone in the world who could ever have a thing to boast of. Nothing really belonged to us. We were merely trustees for the short period of time we spend here on earth—trustees of our time, talents, money, our heart and affections and physical bodies. That was quite a lesson for a seventeen-year-old to learn, and I took it to heart.

The second passage I memorized is probably the most meaningful verse in the Bible to Christians everywhere: "For God so loved the world, that he gave his only begotten Son, that whosoever believeth in him should not perish, but have everlasting life" (John 3:16). I believe, firmly, that this is the most wonderful gift of all time. It is beyond my understanding why God, who knows all, sees all and is all powerful should love us—who have all sinned against him. Love us so much that he gave his only begotten, perfect son as an atonement for the sins of all those who simply but sincerely accept his son Jesus Christ as their personal Saviour and Lord.

The third passage was: "Trust in the Lord with all thine heart; and lean not unto thine own understanding. In all thy ways acknowledge him and he shall direct thy paths" (Proverbs 3:5,6).

I have learned, since then, that the trouble we get into in life occurs only if we don't trust in God—if we lean on our own understanding. I was fortunate to learn that early; I avoided a lot of trouble. Following my conversion to Christ, during the days in which I searched the Bible and memorized portions that were particularly meaningful to me, my life took on a whole new direction quickly—a direction that has blessed me far more than I deserve.

All of the things I learned as a youngster in Pickford didn't come directly out of the Bible—some things I had to learn the hard way. The Bible teaches us the same things painlessly, but before I took my Bible seriously—when I was twelve or thirteen —I was given my first .22 rifle. I decided I'd go down to the river and shoot a wild duck. As luck would have it, I shot my duck, and then, proud as I could be, I paraded down the main street of Pickford—duck in one hand, rifle in the other.

By the time I got opposite the town hotel, one of the men sitting on the porch yelled out that the game warden was in town and he'd soon be after me. "You shot that duck out of season!" he said.

Naturally, I was half-scared to death. I ran all the way home, buried the duck in the backyard and hid in the hayloft for the rest of the day! "Knowing the law" was a lesson I learned that day, and it is one of the reasons why I have been in court only twice in my life: Once because a man forged my name to a check, and I had to appear to testify; the second time I was asked to provide information to help the court reach a decision in a matter that didn't involve me or my business.

With God's guidance and help, I have tried hard to stay within the law. And I've insisted that my businesses operate in accord with the law. I have never forgotten the day I shot that duck out of season and, as a result, my life has been more peaceful and less complicated. That day has enabled me to proceed better toward goals that really mean something. Some young people today don't realize what they're doing to themselves when they deliberately defy the law. Just one mistake can follow them for the rest of their lives: It's on the record and can pop up to spoil the prospect of a good job; it can cast aspersions on their characters at the most unexpected moments.

I had four sisters and two brothers and, because my mother was determined we have a good education, six of us graduated from college, and one brother finished a two-year technical course in Chicago. If you consider that our little town of Pickford didn't even have a high school—we had to go to Sault Sainte Marie, about twenty-five miles away—you can see just how wonderful and determined my mother really was!

We didn't have automobiles in those days, so I had to live in Sault Sainte Marie during the school year, and I had to earn most of my own living. I was a Western Union messenger my first year in high school, and I studied telegraphy nights. In my second year, I was made telegraph operator!

During that summer I worked in Soo Junction as a relief operator on the Duluth, South Shore and Atlantic Railroad, allowing the regular operator to take his vacation. One very rainy night a freight train pulled in, headed west for Marquette, and I guess I made maybe the biggest mistake of my life. The fear I experienced, and the lesson I learned, may have played some part in bringing me to Christ the following year, because the Lord gave me a mighty important second chance, that rainy night at Soo Junction.

When the train arrived, the conductor and engineer told me they were going up to the yards to pick up some freight cars. They said they'd come back to the station to pick up water at the water tank. In the meantime, the train dispatcher sent me a train order, directing the freight train to pull off onto a siding about forty miles up the track. This order was called a "31 Order," and it demanded the signature of both the conductor and the engineer. In addition, before that train was allowed to leave, I had to report back to the dispatcher that the order had been signed.

Well—I looked out the window at the miserable weather; I looked at the 31 Order. After all, I *knew* the train was coming back to the water tank and that practically all I'd have to do would be reach out the window and hand them the "31 Order," without having to run into the yards and get soaked. So—I telegraphed the dispatcher that the order had been signed.

Then I waited for the train to return. I waited—and I waited —and I waited! Then it occurred to me that maybe they *weren't* coming back! That was a sickening feeling. I dashed out into the

28

rain; there was the train pulling out onto the mainline, going west to Marquette. They had decided not to come back to the station for water.

I don't remember if I prayed, but I do know I ran as fast as my legs would carry me: *The reason this particular freight train was being ordered off onto the siding was to let a special passenger train go by that was headed for the State Fair in Detroit. If I couldn't get the order to them, a terrible accident was inevitable!*

By the grace of God, I reached the train in time, presented the order, and a tragedy was averted. I had lied in telling the dispatcher that the order had been signed, and never—as long as I live—will I ever again doubt the wisdom of the countless passages in the Bible that are concerned with telling the truth. I can't say that I've never told a lie since that rainy night, but the Lord had made me aware of truth in such a dramatic way it has remained in the forefront of my consciousness to this day. When, with the Lord's help, I authored *The Four-Way Test*, the first test, "Is it the truth?" needed no special prompting.

These were some of the important experiences I had as a boy—experiences that helped mold my life and drew me nearer to the Lord in humbleness and belief. I went on to graduate from Northwestern University in 1917, with a Bachelor of Science degree. Then, I served with the YMCA and the U.S. Navy in France.

I had found Christ, but I still had no definite plan for my life. Not until after the war was over did I have that talk with George Perkins—the one I told you about in the first chapter—and God's plan for me emerged. God has a plan for you, too, if you'll seek it sincerely. Some of the experiences I had, while I was following my plan were mighty interesting.

3

"Sign 'em up" Days

I WAS MARRIED in Chicago in 1919 to Gloria Forbrich, daughter of Charles and Rovilla Forbrich. My wife and I went down to Paul's Valley, Oklahoma, a town of about 5,000 people—where Sinclair Oil Company had assigned me as timekeeper and assistant to the General Manager on the construction of a pipeline station. Sinclair had told us that we would be in Paul's Valley only about a year—just enough time to learn the pipeline end of the business. When the year was up, and we were readying ourselves to leave for my next Sinclair assignment, a wildcat outfit brought in an oil well—the first one in Garvin County—and local interest in oil really took a jump.

I decided to resign from Sinclair and go into the oilfield business as a lease broker. I opened up a combination lease-brokerage, insurance and real estate office and soon became involved in every phase of the county's life—especially in Paul's Valley, which was the county seat.

Following the plan I believed God had given me, I devoted whatever spare time I had to community, and especially youth activities. Although Gloria and I attended the Methodist Church, we noted that the local Presbyterian Church was a dilapidated old building. There was real concern in the community that it might literally fall apart.

I figured that if we moved over to the Presbyterian Church, we might be able to bring more people into the church and thus raise funds for a new building. Fortunately, it worked out that way, and I began to understand more fully that if the Lord wants something done, it can be done. The Presbyterian Church installed me as a teacher of the men's class. We attracted a number of new members, and I became Chairman of the Finance Committee. Thanks to the Lord, and many enthusiastic church members, we got ourselves a new $65,000 church.

My business in Paul's Valley prospered right from the start, especially the lease-brokerage part of it, but I wasn't doing too well in the life insurance business. Speaking to my wife, one night at dinner, I criticized a fellow because he wouldn't buy life insurance from me.

Gloria turned to me and said: "Herb, I'd like to ask you just two questions. First, does the man really need insurance?"

"Of course he does," I said. "He has a $10,000 loan on his buildings. He has a wife and three children, and he has only $2,000 in life insurance."

"All right," said Gloria, "here's the second question: Does he have enough money to pay for the premium?"

I said he did.

Then Gloria said to me: "You know what I think? I think you're to blame for not selling him the policy. It's not his fault for not buying."

That straight answer changed my entire outlook on selling. What my wife was saying was that if a man needed a product, and could afford to buy it, it was strictly up to the ability of the salesman to make the sale.

I knew this man needed the additional life insurance as protection for his wife and children. (Only a short time before, God had blessed my wife and me with a wonderful baby girl, whom we named Beverly. I had taken out additional life insurance at that time.) I knew, also, that he had the money to pay the premiums. So I went back to him again and again—and finally sold him a $10,000 policy.

31

During the previous six months, I had sold only $100,000 worth of life insurance, but in the six months after that quiet talk with Gloria, I sold more than $600,000 worth of life insurance, won The Travelers Insurance Company's Southwestern sales contest for that period *and* a one-month trip to Quebec, Canada, with Gloria. In the three years I sold life insurance in Paul's Valley, I was one of the largest producers in the state of Oklahoma; I believe my final sales total was about $1,500,000.

I don't take any credit for this, because the things that go into successful selling are the product of God-given talent and experience. The experiences I had had before coming to Paul's Valley were the kind that dealt with truth, knowing the law, assuming proper responsibility and, most of all, doing business in accord with Biblical precepts of honesty and forthrightness. If you think this statement sounds as if I was almost continually conscious of the Lord in all of my dealings with my fellowmen, you're absolutely right, for this attitude showed itself in my community involvement. A lot of things needed doing in Paul's Valley—for the sake of the community and, especially the young people; because I had the time and the enthusiasm, I figured the Lord was just waiting for me to get on with the job.

The Chamber of Commerce in Paul's Valley was in debt. Furthermore, many of the local businessmen had little interest in the community. The first job, then, was to get the Chamber of Commerce out of debt and to give the town back some of its pride so that some useful projects could be started. I was named Secretary of the Chamber of Commerce and, because the Chamber couldn't afford my salary, I donated it; within about five months, the Chamber was finally out of debt.

One of the big needs in those days was paved roads. Automobiles had come of age, and Garvin County didn't have one foot of paved highway. This slowed business down and gave the town an unhealthy backwoods image. I realized the need for paved roads, so a new secretary was appointed to the Chamber, and I spent much of my nonbusiness time signing up names in favor of a roads bond issue.

The Daily Oklahoman, in its issue of December 28, 1924, carried a full-page illustrated article on the controversial road issue, and headlined it: "SIGN 'EM UP TAYLOR OF PAUL'S VALLEY." It amuses me to read that article today, because I guess that's just what I was. The same lesson I learned about salesmanship from my wife, I applied to all of the community projects in which I got involved, and I guess the people in Paul's Valley remembered me best as a young man with a petition in his hand.

We later got the roads we wanted—the bond issue passed by a three-to-one margin—but that was only one of the activities the Lord led me into in Paul's Valley. There were others that I believe were even more important: I was privileged to help organize the first Boy Scout Troop in the town, the Hi-Y club in the high school, the annual Boys' and Girls' week and the Boys' Work Council. The young people, our greatest asset, were being neglected, and, of course, this kind of work was closest to my heart and to my lifelong plan.

It was also in Garvin County that I first became connected with Rotary. The Rotary Club is a community builder as well as a confidence builder, and I didn't think my job would be finished in Garvin County if the largest cities in the county didn't each have a good Rotary Club. Paul's Valley and Wynnewood were active rivals for the farmer's trade, and I felt that if we had a Rotary Club in Wynnewood, as well as in Paul's Valley, we would be able to secure closer cooperation in attaining projects for the common good of both cities, such as the securing of hard-surfaced roads! Later on in this book, I will have more to say about Rotary and why I believe it is one of the strongest and most meaningful institutions in the world; for now, it is enough to say that we got the Rotary Club established in Wynnewood, and the spirit and machinery to keep Garvin County on an upward course seemed to be about complete. According to a promise I had made my wife, we were scheduled to move to Chicago after spending five years in Paul's Valley: The time had come to fulfill that promise.

While I was in Paul's Valley, I let it be known to certain Chicago businessmen that I would be leaving the area soon. I received several job offers—one, of course, from the Travelers Insurance Company. The Travelers position was tempting, but Maurice H. Karker, a man I had served under in the Navy, and who was then president of the Jewel Tea Company in Chicago, told me he'd take me into his company and move me along as fast as I was able to move, starting off as office manager. I prayed about the matter, and I seemed to have a definite leading to go with Mr. Karker. I liked the man, knew his reputation and had a lot of confidence in him.

I told Mr. Karker I'd take the job. I knew I had turned down a good salary with Travelers, but I had no idea what Mr. Karker was going to give me; we had never discussed it.

When I showed up for work the first day, Mr. Karker said: "Why, you don't even know how much I'm going to pay you."

"I'm not concerned," I said. "All I care about is that you'll move me along as fast as I'm ready and able to move along."

That surprised Mr. Karker, and he laughed.

"I want you to know," he said, "you're the first man I have ever hired who didn't know what his beginning salary was to be!"

The four and a half years I spent in Paul's Valley, Oklahoma, enriched my experiences immeasurably. I had prospered in business and, according to God's plan, had been able to devote my spare time to worthwhile community projects. Many of the things I learned were to be of great help to me in future years, and I'm convinced that the Lord led me to Paul's Valley so I would be better equipped, mentally and spiritually, to overcome the many difficult problems that lay ahead of me in selling, organizing, financing, and attaining group cooperation and effort in countless business, community and religious projects.

Often, when I'm asked about the hardest sale I ever made, my thoughts go back to Paul's Valley. Actually, it wasn't a sale at all, but a purchase, and I think it's appropriate to finish this chapter on those wonderful days in Paul's Valley with this interesting story.

Another oil man and I set out one morning to buy an oil lease on a farm located in the center of a block of acreage. (A large oil company wanted to drill a wildcat oil well in the center of this farm. They had tried and tried to buy the lease, but the owner refused to sell. The oil company finally asked me to try to buy the lease for them.) As we entered the gates of the farm, the deputy sheriff was leaving. The deputy had just served notice on the man that his wife was suing him for divorce. We knew that we could not get our lease unless we had her signature. The natural thing for a salesman to do in a case of this sort would be to return to town and await developments. Then the thought occurred to me that more important than securing the oil lease was keeping that home together and the family intact.

Was there any way I might be able to help heal the breach between the farmer and his wife? It turned out there was. The couple had six small children, and, using these as the "need" for the reconciliation, we finally got the farmer in our car, and took him to a neighbor's house, where his wife was staying. Then we held a little divorce trial all of our own and took them both home happy. We got the oil lease signed up and started for town with a slip of paper, asking a certain Paul's Valley attorney to call off the divorce suit.

As I said, we had some wonderful days in Paul's Valley.

4

The 4 Way Test

THE ULTIMATE objective in life is to know and obey God's will for you—His plan for you. It doesn't take much imagination to realize the strength and satisfaction that can come into your life if you're directed by God. Everything becomes purposeful, your enthusiasm and energy are boundless, and everything you accomplish is in accord with a higher plan, and therefore is lasting and productive. Though no mortal man may remember your name, the man or woman who follows God's will is literally immortal in God's memory, and you have God's assurance that your salvation is sealed. Surely, there can be no wiser purpose in life than to seek and know God's plan for you. I had an inkling of the plan for my life, but I didn't know how quickly and dramatically it was going to begin to unfold when I returned to Chicago and joined the Jewel Tea Company.

Thanks to the many things I'd learned in my selling experiences in Paul's Valley, I made quick progress at Jewel. If you like selling you can make almost any selling effort a most interesting experience.

Let me illustrate this point, with an excerpt from an article that appeared in 1954—in the now defunct *American* magazine:

> *I recall a young salesman for a widely known grocery firm which sold its goods from door to door. Making the*

rounds one day in Tulsa, Okla., he knocked on the door of a bungalow and asked the woman who opened it if Mrs. Wilson was home. (Of course, he'd known enough to pick up the name of the lady of the house while making his previous call next door.)

"I'm sorry, but Mrs. Wilson's in bed," he was told.

If the young man had been thinking only of making a sale, he might have given up at that point. Instead, he said, "I'm sorry, too. What's the trouble?"

"Well, it's not trouble exactly," said the woman at the door. "She had a baby and isn't up and around yet."

"That's wonderful!" the salesman exclaimed. "My wife just had a girl. I'd love to see Mrs. Wilson's baby if she'd let me."

In a moment he was inside admiring the newcomer—also a girl—who lay in a crib next to the mother's bed. "What's her name?" he asked.

"My husband and I haven't thought of a name we like," Mrs. Wilson said. "It's quite a problem."

"Maybe I can help you," the salesman said. "We called our baby Ramona."

Mrs. Wilson said she liked the name and would suggest it to her husband. The salesman was about to leave. "By the way," Mrs. Wilson asked, "how did you happen to call?"

"I came to tell you about our coffee and tea, and explain the premium plan," he said.

By this time Mrs. Wilson and the other woman felt that the salesman was a friend, because he'd been interested in the thing closest to their hearts—the new baby. Before he left, they were both marked down as customers, and a few days later he got a letter saying that the baby's name was Ramona.

I know this story because I was the young man in question. Today my daughters, Beverly and Ramona, are grown women with children of their own, but every passing year *has strengthened my belief that thinking of others, or "service above self," combined with hard work, not only are the rules for good living and good citizenship, but in the long run bring the richest returns.*

I moved along rapidly at Jewel Tea—first as Home Office Manager, then as Assistant to the President, then Vice President. By 1929, I was a member of the Board of Directors and, in 1930, I became Executive Vice President of the company, just one notch below Mr. Karker, the President. My salary and bonuses at this time amounted to about $33,000 a year and, in those days, there were no income taxes. I mention my earnings only because of the events that were to follow—events that demonstrate that if you know and follow God's plan for you, everything works for the best, regardless of any temporary sacrifice you may have to make.

I was in line for the presidency of Jewel Tea, when a vice president of the Continental National Bank in Chicago asked Mr. Karker if he would allow me to spend half of my time helping another company stay out of bankruptcy—the Club Aluminum Products Company. I had charge of merchandising as well as manufacturing at Jewel and had made a good record— good enough that the bankers felt I might be the fellow to step into the failing Club Aluminum, save the company from collapse and safeguard the jobs of about 250 people employed there. In 1930, in the grim days of the "Great Depression," millions of men were out of jobs, companies were going bankrupt everywhere you looked; even banks were failing. It was an immensely serious and difficult period in our country's history, and thousands of men of my generation have made it part of their life's work to assure, as well as anything of this nature *can* be assured, that the present generation will not have to face the same chaos.

Mr. Karker agreed that Club Aluminum could contract for half of my time, so I went to that company, along with some other fellows I'd selected. After we had gotten all of the facts on the table and had settled up the law suits pending against the company, we found that the company was $400,000 in debt! Club Aluminum owed that much more than it had in assets, and any three creditors could have gotten together and thrown the company into bankruptcy. It was a bleak picture, to put it mildly and, when we turned in our report to the Creditors Committee, they advised us to close up the doors. By now it was 1932—the year some economists call the depth of the depression—there didn't seem to be any way to save Club Aluminum and to keep the employees on the job.

Mr. Karker agreed that Club Aluminum could not be saved and asked me to come back full-time to Jewel Tea, but something strange was going on inside of me. When I compared that wonderful $33,000-a-year job at Jewel with the almost impossible financial position of Club Aluminum, the thought occurred to me, "Is this where God really wants me?"

The brief experience with Club Aluminum had been somewhat exciting—facing difficult, almost impossible situations, asking the Lord for guidance, then seeing how He gave the answer of what to do. Could it be that the Lord wanted me to go to the Club Aluminum Company as president?

I did a lot of praying about it. Naturally, nobody thought it would be a wise move, but I couldn't shake the feeling that God's plan for me was to make the move. It seemed to me *this* was the company He'd chosen for me to fulfill the second part of the original plan—being with a company where, in the future, I might influence the setting of policies that would enable me to give more and more of my time directly to the Lord's work.

Well, I was confident I was being directed by God, so I really didn't have any choice. With natural trepidation, but also with growing enthusiasm for the challenge that lay ahead, I turned in my resignation to Jewel Tea, borrowed $6,100 on some of my Jewel Tea stock and, after some necessary corporate reorganizing, wound up as President of the Club Aluminum Products Company at a salary of $6,000 a year. At that time, it was quite apparent that I was the only person convinced that the company could be saved. I was convinced because the Holy Spirit told me so. And here, let me refer to John 16:13 where what Jesus told his disciples is recorded: "Howbeit when he the Spirit of truth is come, he will guide you into all truth . . . and he will show you things to come."

Many articles have been written about "The Four-Way Test". It is made up of twenty-four words I wrote in 1932, after sincere prayer. These words are not only responsible, to a great degree, for the success of the Club Aluminum Products Company, but they are also credited with changing the lives of hundreds of thousands of people all over the world. I can't think of a better place to retell that story than right here and, as you read, I ask all of you to consider carefully the way things can work out well for you if you place yourself in the hands of God's wisdom and let yourself be guided by His will in even the most difficult circumstances. If you will let yourself be guided by honesty, fairness, a spirit of goodwill—these fundamental Christian values— calling upon Christ and the guidance of the Holy Spirit for further understanding and belief, you will be on the right path, with the blessing of knowing God's plan for you. You will become a thousandfold more productive than you could ever be without God, as this story of "The Four-Way Test" will verify.

Ever since my days in Paul's Valley, I've known that what God wants to be done *can* be done. I knew He didn't want 250 people to lose their jobs and the pay they had coming to them, when they could not get jobs elsewhere. I was convinced He had placed me in Club Aluminum for a definite purpose. The first job, then, was to set policies for the company that would reflect the high ethics and morals God would want in any business. If the people who worked for Club Aluminum were to *think right*, I knew they would *do right*. What we needed was a simple, easily remembered guide to right conduct—a sort of ethical yardstick— which all of us in the company could memorize and apply to what we thought, said and did in our relations with others.

I searched through many books for the answer to our need, but the right phrases eluded me, so I did what I often do when I have a problem I can't answer myself: I turn to the One who has all the answers. I leaned over my desk, rested my head in my hands, and prayed. After a few moments, I looked up and reached for a white paper card. Then I wrote down the twenty-four words that had come to me:

1. Is is the truth?
2. Is it fair to all concerned?
3. Will it build goodwill and better friendships?
4. Will it be beneficial to all concerned?

I called it "The Four-Way Test" of the things we think, say or do.

I decided to apply the first test, "Is it the truth?" to everything that came up that day in the office. The first thing that crossed my desk was a tearsheet of some advertising, in which our products were billed as "the greatest cookware in the world." I knew we couldn't prove a statement like that. Furthermore, there was no way of knowing if it were true.

I called in the Advertising Manager and instructed him to eliminate superlatives from all future advertising. No more would we be using words like "best" or "finest" or "greatest," not even phrases such as "better than another brand."

"From now on," I told him, "we will only tell the facts as we know them about our product."

After thinking about The Four-Way Test for about two months, and applying it to a number of business problems and situations, I called in my four department heads to discuss it with them. One of these men was a Roman Catholic, another a Christian Scientist, another an Orthodox Jew, and the fourth a Presbyterian.

I asked them if there were anything in The Four-Way Test that was contrary to their religious or moral beliefs.

Each of the men studied the text carefully, then said, "No." They agreed to memorize it and use it.

The next step was to inform everyone in the company of The Four-Way Test and to encourage them to apply it to everything they thought, said and did in their business relations with others. The Four-Way Test was now a policy of the Club Aluminum Products Company. We had the right to insist that they use the test in our business, and we were hopeful our employees would use it in their private lives as well.

At times The Four-Way Test was hard to live up to—considering that we had very little cash; the company was still bankrupt and we were in the midst of a national depression. One of our top salesmen came in one day—a man whose judgement I respected—and said that The Four-Way Test was going to play havoc with our sales.

"Our procedure" he said, "has always been to sell a dealer as much as we can, even if we load him down with our product." The dealer usually bought more than was good for him, carrying a larger inventory than he needed and, as a result, he was forced to push our products to customers who might not want or need them.

"Your procedure doesn't agree with point number three in The Four-Way Test as far as I can see," I told the salesman. "It won't build goodwill with either the dealer or the final customer. And it certainly doesn't agree with point number four, 'Will it be beneficial to all concerned?' "

Then I told him to try selling according to The Four-Way Test. I suggested it would be more profitable in the long run.

Not only did we put The Four-Way Test into practice with our salesmen, we printed The Four-Way Test on the backs of our calling cards. Our salesmen were instructed to say something like this: "Of course, I can't live up to this perfectly, but I'd appreciate your help. Whenever you find I'm not living up to it, let me know, and I'll do my best to change."

The test worked wonders. Instead of persuading a dealer to take more merchandise than he needed, the salesman helped the dealer determine what he could reasonably expect to sell. Then the salesman gave him tips and other material to *help* him sell it.

It goes without saying that we began winning renewed confidence from our dealers. This feeling was passed along by the dealers to the eventual customers, and sales began to climb steadily.

Another time, we were put to *our own* test in applying The Four-Way Test. Our sales manager bounded in the door one day, breathlessly announcing a possible order for more than 50,000 utensils! It was summertime and sales were low, so we were still in a bankrupt condition. We certainly needed and wanted that tremendous business!

But, there was a hitch. Our sales manager, after thinking a moment about The Four-Way Test, said that his potential customer intended to sell our products at cut-rate prices. "This wouldn't be fair to our regular dealers, who have been advertising and promoting our products consistently," the sales manager continued, "who always sell at a set price, which we agree is fair to all."

We turned the order down—probably the most difficult thing we had to do in those early bankrupt days. But there was no question that this particular business transaction would have made a mockery out of The Four-Way Test principles we lived by.

Once, we gave a job to a printer, because his bid was $500 lower than competing bids. When we received the printed material, the printer said that he had made a $500 mistake in his estimate and would we be willing to make up his loss?

The last thing our company had was a spare $500! Our executives conferred on the matter, and one of them said, "We acted in good faith—let the printer take his loss."

Another man said, "But that may not agree with point number two in The Four-Way Test. If the printer made an honest mistake, then it will not be *fair to all concerned* if we penalize him. Let's find out, first, if it *was* an honest mistake."

A little checking convinced us the printer's error was not deliberate; we gave him the $500. Without The Four-Way Test, I doubt that we would have.

By practicing The Four-Way Test as faithfully as possible, we built good will among our competitors as well as our dealers and consumers. We refused to knock a competitive product. In fact, we tried to make certain that we never spoke about our competitors unless we had something good to say. By applying The Four-Way Test and by speaking well of our competitors when a compliment was warranted, our entire industry grew in the esteem of dealers and consumers alike. And that meant more sales for all of us.

This combination of God's help, The Four-Way Test—which came in answer to prayer—good people and good products, enabled us to cancel our $400,000 debt within five years. We paid it off with interest—every single dollar of it! In the early days, some of our creditors would have been happy to settle for ten cents on the dollar, but we didn't want them to lose their money. We asked them to be patient; they were, and they got paid in full.

During the next fifteen years, we distributed over one million dollars in stock dividends and the net worth of the company climbed to over one million, seven hundred and fifty thousand dollars. The original $6100, which I had borrowed on my Jewel Tea stock when I joined Club Aluminum Company, and which I had put into the business, was the only money we had borrowed or invested in that miraculous twenty-year span.

By soliciting God's help prayerfully, in deciding between my job with Jewel Tea and the Club Aluminum Company, and by praying for His help in formulating the basic policies of the Club Aluminum Company—the prayer that resulted in The Four-Way Test—I was asking for God's guidance in my business life. Can any person reading this book doubt seriously that I received God's aid in great measure?

But that, of course, was only part of it. It is in our *personal* lives that The Four-Way Test is most beneficial and meaningful. And, if we hadn't used the success of our business to further emphasize The Four-Way Test and our dependence upon God's principles, morals and ethics, our business success would have been hollow indeed.

Widespread publicity for The Four-Way Test, however, was not to come until the early 1940's. Then it was used worldwide in offices, schools, homes and organizations of many kinds . . . but I'll tell you about that later. For the moment, let's return to those first years when Club Aluminum was struggling to survive. As you may remember, the second part of God's plan for me was to get into a business where I could control the company and could influence the setting of policies that would enable me to have time for Christian work.

Now, I was able to get away from the business part-time; The Four-Way Test had been created; and, although I couldn't predict the great scope of success that my business eventually realized, God knew all about it, and He felt it was time to introduce me to the work that would, eventually, claim my full time. I arranged for my salary to be reduced to cover only the time I worked for the company and started to work on Christian character-building projects for youth.

Whoever you are, whatever your situation in life, it is doubtful you could ever be as hopeless or underprivileged or as seemingly without purpose or promise in this life as some of the young people I am going to tell you about now.

Yet many of them rose out of chaos and disorder to become happy, productive men and women, with the sense of pride, satisfaction and dignity every person needs and wants desperately.

They found a plan for their lives, and the story is dramatic and exciting.

5

A Plan Unfolds

WHEN I CAME up to Chicago from Paul's Valley, my interest in church and community affairs continued as strongly as ever. In Paul's Valley, almost all of my non-business time was devoted to helping youth. In addition to the activities I've described—the Boy Scouts and Hi-Y—as President of the Paul's Valley Rotary Club, I helped organize a special program, in which boys in the state correctional institution could spend some time in the homes of Rotary members. This Rotary program was exceptionally beneficial. I believe we reduced by 40 percent the number of boys who, normally, got back into trouble after they were released. When boys were released from the state institution, we arranged for Rotary Clubs in particular towns or cities to keep an eye on the youngsters and to help them progress.

The important part of this activity was that it enabled me to get acquainted with all types of young people: the neglected boy, the delinquent boy, the wealthy boy as well as the poor boy, the farm boy, the city boy—all kinds of boys. And my experience with them was not superficial; it was deep and rewarding. It gave me insight into the real problems of young people, and I learned a great deal about the kinds of programs and methods needed to help these boys in cities, towns and villages.

I brought this experience with me to Chicago, and I became involved in many community and church projects, one of which was teaching a Sunday-school class of high-school students. All of this activity was meaningful, but my thoughts kept going, more and more, toward the Near North Side of Chicago—a very poor district.

My wife Gloria and I were keenly aware of the acute poverty and deprivation of the Near North Side. Even for depression days, the people in this section of Chicago were markedly destitute. Many of them didn't have warm clothes or enough to eat.

In the early 1930's, my wife and I set up a small storefront mission. We arranged for some Chicago bakeries to give the mission bread. The news spread, and before long we had hundreds of people standing in line, waiting for the bread and the soup the mission provided. Men, women and children stood in line for hours and hours in the coldest weather—just to get something to eat. Those were difficult days indeed.

As part of the mission program, we had a full-time minister, who conducted evangelistic services and a Sunday school for the youngsters.

When we started talking with the children, we realized right away that the only Christian instruction most of them were receiving was right here at the mission. They weren't getting it at home; they weren't getting it at church. We made a survey of the 2,000 homes around the mission and found that about 50 percent of the children in the area didn't go to any church or Sunday school.

Then we made a second survey to find out why this situation existed. We talked with mothers and fathers, and we found many reasons. Some parents said they couldn't afford to buy the kind of clothes their children needed to attend Sunday school. Others said they didn't have any interest in the church. Still others said the church they had attended did not hold their interest.

Eventually, we reached a conclusion: A tremendous challenge was being set before us—to help the church reach these thousands of young people. We knew that the situation in the Near North Side was being repeated all over the country—in other cities like New York, Philadelphia and Los Angeles. What was needed, we decided, were nondenominational organizations that could provide a Christian witness to these children, and their parents, in a way they could understand and accept. We had to provide organizations and people who could reach unchurched children and, eventually, funnel them into the church of their choice.

My wife and I did a lot of praying about this matter. By 1940, with the Club Aluminum Products Company progressing rapidly, we knew it was time to put our convictions into action. God had shown us the need; now he had provided the means to answer it.

Our first act was to set up a nonprofit foundation—The Christian Workers Foundation. I gave 25 percent of the Club Aluminum Company's stock to the foundation and, of course, the dividends earned by the stock supplied the capital to run the foundation. I was forty-seven years old in 1940, and if you remember the original three-part plan designed for my life, this should be about the time I was destined to begin spending more time on community and religious projects than in my business. (The original trustees of the Christian Workers Foundation were my wife Gloria, Lysle Smith, our attorney, and myself. Through the years, my dear friend Lysle Smith has contributed all of the needed legal services involved in a number of nonprofit organizations we helped to organize.)

It was working out that way exactly. There was such a tremendous challenge facing The Christian Workers Foundation. If it were to accomplish the goals we had set for it, it required some of my time and energy; I gave it gladly and enthusiastically.

Shortly after the foundation was organized, through an interview arranged by Stacey Woods, I arranged to go to Toronto to meet with officers of the Canadian branch of the organization, IVCF (Inter-Varsity Christian Fellowship). It was a British organization and, except for a chapter at the University of Michigan, did not have an organization in the United States. The reason I wanted to talk to them was because I believed our first activity in the Christian Workers Foundation should be to reach the college-level young people—the ones about to go out into the world and into business, where they could be influential in the Lord's work. They were in the prime of life. They had received their training and were ready to produce results. In other words, we wanted to help found and support an organization that would reach unchurched college students. IVCF seemed to be just what we wanted.

While I was in Toronto, I asked the IVCF Board to give us Stacey Woods—half of his time, at least—to help us organize IVCF in the United States. They agreed, and Stacey Woods and I started from scratch back in the Chicago offices of the Christian Workers Foundation in 1940.

We set up IVCF of the United States on a $10,000 budget for the first year. The foundation donated $6,500 and the remaining $3,500 came from public donations. That was a pretty small beginning for an organization that, in 1966, for example, received about $700,000 from more than 25,000 people all over the country.

Today, of course, IVCF of the United States is the largest college student evangelistic project in the world and has chapters or other activities on more than 700 college campuses.

As many of you may know, IVCF of the United States later merged with Foreign Missions Fellowship, which is composed of groups from Christian colleges who plan to go into foreign countries as missionaries. The Christian Nurses Fellowship also merged with IVCF. These girls meet in medical schools and in hospitals. Today, we have over one hundred chapters.

An illustration of the spirit of IVCF and the great acceptance this wonderful Christian organization has had since its emergence in the United States is the fact that more than 7,200 college students gave up their Christmas vacations and paid their own expenses, to attend an IVCF-sponsored missionary conference at Illinois University between Christmas and New Year in 1967.

Now of course this kind of thing doesn't hit the newspaper

headlines. There were articles in a few magazines about it, but not many people in the United States were aware of these wonderful, dedicated young men and women and of their desire to serve the Lord.

Back in 1940, though, we didn't know how greatly our heavenly Father was going to bless Inter-Varsity Christian Fellowship in the United States. It was the first major venture Christian Workers Foundation helped to pioneer, and it represented our hopes for reaching unchurched college students with the gospel message of Christ. Even as we started the IVCF program, we had other plans for reaching high-school-age youngsters. These plans ran right on down the line through junior-high school and the elementary grades—even the preschool years. Our experiences in the Near North Side of Chicago became indelibly engraved on my mind, and on Gloria's. With God's help, whose plan was clearly before us to follow, we intended to help pioneer and finance the nondenominational organizations we felt would do the best job of reaching these young people with the Lord's word.

We offered not only financial help but business and organizational aid—the know-how to assure practical success to organizations guided by men with strong ideals and convictions, who also needed sound business judgement to guarantee the furtherance of their goals. It seems they needed us, and we needed them.

It was a combination destined, with God's blessing, to work miracles during the coming years—in many more areas than we had originally planned.

But there was another reason for beginning the Christian Workers Foundation. This reason, too, met with success far beyond our original hopes.

6

A Test
for All Times

ABOUT TWO YEARS after I had written The Four-Way Test, I found out just why it was written as it was. It had come in answer to prayer, so I was really not too surprised to read—in the Book of Jeremiah—God's own original version of The Four-Way Test. Jeremiah was one of the great prophets and, near the end of his career on earth, he received a message directly from God that was to be given to his people—verses 23-24 of chapter 9 [author's italics]:

> Thus saith the Lord, "Let not the wise man glory in his wisdom, neither let the mighty man glory in his might, let not the rich man glory in his riches; But let him that glorieth glory in this, that he understandeth and knoweth me, that I am the Lord, which exercise *loving kindness*, [*justice*] *and righteousness* in the earth; for in these things I delight, saith the Lord.

Loving kindness is covered by the questions: "Will it build goodwill and better friendships?" and "Will it be beneficial to all concerned?"

Justice is covered by the question: "Is it fair to all concerned?"

Righteousness is covered in the first question of The Four-Way Test: "Is it the truth?"

51

Every time we think of The Four-Way Test, then, and every time we apply it to our thoughts, words and deeds, we are really fulfilling "these things" in which God delights.

This passage of Scripture reminds us that our heavenly Father tells us *not* to glory in getting a better education, a higher position in life, or more money. After all, these are temporal values which end at the grave. He tells us that the things he delights in are the eternal values of truth, justice and love of our fellowman. Knowing this, and seeing how miraculously The Four-Way Test had proved beneficial in business and personal life, we decided to further its publication and use through the Christian Workers Foundation. The Four-Way Test has, since then, been accepted by all religious faiths, by people of every race and political attachment in the free countries of the world. It was easy to read and remember; it appealed to the good in all people; and its brevity made it easy to reproduce on cards, plaques and other ways that were practical and handy in speeding up its wide acceptance and use.

Furthering the use of The Four-Way Test through the Christian Workers Foundation was the beginning of its worldwide acceptance. But, when we gave the right to use it to Rotary International, in 1942, things really started to happen!

We turned over the right at a Rotary Club meeting, at which I was telling how the test came to me in answer to prayer, and how it had helped me in personal and business life. One of the men in the audience asked if he could jot it down. Several other people took pen and paper and copied it as I repeated it.

One of the members of the Board of Directors of Rotary International asked if that organization might use the test to promote Rotary's objectives of high ethical standards. Certainly, I had no objections. In 1954, when I was President of Rotary International, I presented the copyright to them. The rights to use The Four-Way Test were retained for Christian Workers Foundation, the Club Aluminum Company and myself.

Today, The Four-Way Test is translated into the language of

more than a hundred countries. It sits on the desks—in the form of a plaque—of more than 450,000 leading business and professional men in America alone. Each school day, over 3,000,000, high-school students see The Four-Way Test displayed on large posters on the front walls of their classrooms. It is in poster form in high schools and colleges in twenty-five other countries. One city, Daytona Beach, Florida, used The Four-Way Test in a citywide plan: Posters and placards were erected throughout the city; the test was implemented on radio, newspapers and many other ways. At the end of the first year, Daytona Beach found juvenile delinquency had been reduced by over 20 percent. The divorce rate had gone down; bank earnings and business transactions had increased compared with other communities in the surrounding area; and all other results proved positive.

Part of the Daytona Beach plan included putting little Four-Way Test stickers on automobile windshields. We did this on about 15,000 cars, and the only thing we added to The Four-Way Test itself was the sentence: "How does your driving check with The Four-Way Test?"

Everybody agreed that three of the test questions made sense; but the first question, "Is it the truth?" stumped them. They wanted to know what that had to do with driving.

I said, "That is to be used when the policeman stops you!"

We cut down on a lot of accidents that year in Daytona Beach, and one of the reasons was because drivers felt they must drive more carefully to be fair to others. As a consequence, they probably saved a lot of lives, including their own! Injuries from accidents actually dropped by more than 20 percent during that year period.

As The Four-Way Test gained worldwide acceptance, I found myself being asked to give talks on The Four-Way Test. I obliged as often as possible. Nothing gave me more pleasure than speaking to young people, because I was convinced that the younger a person is the easier it is to correct wrong habits.

Every time I speak to a group of students about The Four-

Way Test, I can't help but be impressed by their tremendous potential. Nobody can tell what a youngster is going to be in ten, fifteen or twenty years. Any group of young people might include a girl who could become one of the great musicians of all time . . . or one of the world's finest artists. Among the boys, there could be a future superintendent of a great metropolitan school system . . . the president of a large corporation, such as General Motors or U.S. Steel . . . even a President of the United States. Nobody can prove to me that these young people will not some day hold these positions. So when I speak before such a distinguished group, I really take it seriously.

I sometimes start my talks by proving to them that at their age they cannot tell what they are going to become. I do it with this little story:

A few years ago, Mrs. Taylor and I were in Japan. We were in Tokyo one day when the telephone rang in our room at the Imperial Hotel. A voice said, "This is Don Hoke."

Well, I remembered Don Hoke. About twenty-two years earlier, he had been a member of my Sunday-school class of high-school boys. I remembered him as being very quiet and unassuming. What do you suppose he said to me on the telephone in Tokyo?

"I want you to come over and visit my college!"

When Mrs. Taylor and I got over there, he asked me to speak, through an interpreter, to the more than 160 students studying for full-time Christian work. Don was not only president of Japan Christian College, he was founder of it! I had no idea that attending my Sunday-school class, twenty-two years before, was a future college president. Nor did I realize that another boy—Allen Mathis, Jr.—would become a vice president of the largest bank in the Midwest and, still later, become my son-in-law and president of my own company, the Club Aluminum Products Company!

54

The first high school in the United States to use The Four-Way Test plan was in Kenosha, Wisconsin. Today, in some states, a majority of the high schools use the test. It is so important in school, in the home, and in business and social life that the earlier youngsters learn The Four-Way Test and apply it to their lives, the better off they'll be.

And I don't mean that it helps them financially, only. Surely, anyone who puts The Four-Way Test into practice in his business—provided he has a good product and good people—will have a better chance at success than without these twenty-four little words: Is it the *truth?* Is it *fair* to all concerned? Will it build *goodwill* and *better friendships?* Will it be *beneficial* to all concerned?

My own business, and the way customers and associates react to our Four-Way Test policy, is proof of its power in business. A man who trusts you will do business with you.

But there is much more to it than that—*reasons* that will help mold a person into a better, more satisfied, more useful human being, no matter what kind of person he is now.

The Four-Way Test, for example, gives a man self-respect when he carries it out. No matter what other people may think of him, *he* knows what he is inside; following The Four-Way Test erases self-doubts and anxieties. He is stronger for it, and he feels he is closer to God and to the ethics and other important characteristics we all yearn for so deeply. In time—without fail —anyone who follows The Four-Way Test faithfully will notice that others think more highly of him also. You can see how important this philosophy is for young people: the earlier they apply the test, the earlier they begin to realize their true potential in whatever field of endeavor they choose to enter.

For example, a youngster who applies The Four-Way Test to his thoughts, words and deeds can become better educated. Someone has said that education is an eternal process of becoming finer, happier and more useful to our fellowman. The Four-

55

Way Test helps us to become finer, happier and more useful and helpful to others. "As a [man] thinketh in his heart, so is he" (Proverbs 23:7). "As a girl thinketh in her heart, so is she." What power there is for good or evil in our thoughts! The Four-Way Test leads our thoughts in the right direction and, therefore, has a strong influence on what we say and do in our relations with others. Every thought we have tends to express itself in actions. What we think is a controlling factor in making us what we are today—in what we are going to become tomorrow. Here is an illustration of how The Four-Way Test influences the thoughts of people:

The Japanese were the first people to use The Four-Way Test in high schools—long before Kenosha, Wisconsin. In Japan, they state things first in the positive, then the negative. They say, for example, "Is it the truth—and never a lie?" "Is it fair to all concerned—and not unfair to anyone?" "Will it build goodwill and better friendships—and no enemies?" "Will it be beneficial to all concerned—and not harmful to anyone?"

At a civic club meeting in a certain city in Japan, a few years ago, one of the members said to the president: "I have a good community service project to recommend. Let us put a big box at the entrance to the railroad station. As you know, quick showers come up, and people get caught in the rain at the railroad station. Let us put a bunch of umbrellas in the box and a sign above it saying: 'Borrow an umbrella and please return this umbrella when you get through with it.' "

A second man got up and said: "Who is going to furnish all the umbrellas? Nobody will ever return those umbrellas."

Then a third man got up and he said: "You know, we have been using The Four-Way Test in our schools, in the form of framed posters in each classroom for the past two years. We have noticed a definite improvement in the moral and ethical standards of our young people. Why not put The Four-Way Test in the umbrellas?"

So, they did. These were big, parchment and bamboo umbrellas, and right on the inside, printed for the borrower to see, was The Four-Way Test (with the added Japanese negatives). At the end of The Four-Way Test, these words were added: "Please return this umbrella to the place where you got it."

At the end of four months, the civic club sent me one of the umbrellas and said that *there wasn't a single umbrella that had not been returned!*

If you go to Japan today, you will find umbrella boxes outside of lots of railroad stations and high schools. The Four-Way Test helped a lot of people to think right. There is a lot of good in everybody; too often we look just for what is bad, instead of looking for the good and encouraging it. The Four-Way Test encourages the good in every person who uses it. It helps people to think right and to think things through before they speak or act. The great poetess Ella Wheeler Wilcox expressed the power of thought in our lives better than I ever can, when she wrote these words:

You never can tell what a thought will do,
In bringing you hate or love.
For thoughts are things, and their airy wings
Are swifter than carrier doves.

They follow the law of the universe,
Each thing creates its kind.
And they speed over the track to bring you back
Whatever went out of your mind.

—You Never Can Tell

Anyone who checks his thoughts, his words and deeds against The Four-Way Test before he expresses himself or takes action is almost certain to do the right thing. People go through life following their strongest thoughts so the challenge is to direct thoughts in the right path.

Sow a thought, and you reap an act; sow an act, and you reap a habit; sow a habit, and you reap a character; sow a character and you reap a destiny."

—*Life and Labor,* Samuel Smiles

Everything starts with right and wrong thinking, and The Four-Way Test—an easy-to-remember modern-day version of God's command to Jeremiah—has proved to be one of the most forceful and rewarding methods of calling thousands of people, young and old, to important and meaningful destinies. It has been called an implementation of the Golden Rule. After all, what would you have others do with you but be sincere? To be fair and just, kind and thoughtful and helpful when you need help?

The Four-Way Test is practiced by millions and it can be truthfully said that it can make anyone's life happier and more successful. When people ask me how to go about using it, I usually suggest that they begin by memorizing it, and then formulate the habit of checking their thoughts, words and deeds with it. Experience with others has shown that the user finds himself doing just that, quickly—and enjoying it—and his relations with others improve steadily. Definitely, it will guide the user in the right direction, toward worthy objectives: choosing, winning and keeping friends; getting along well with others; insuring a happy home life; developing high moral and ethical standards; becoming successful in a chosen business or profession; becoming a better citizen; becoming a better example to the younger people.

This last part—becoming a better example to younger people —is very important, particularly today. All of us exercise influences for good or evil on every young person we meet. At the risk of quoting too many poems, here is one that illustrates what I mean so well that I can't let it go unnoticed:

A careful man (or you could say a careful
*   boy or careful girl)*
I want to be,
A little fellow follows me.
I do not dare to go astray
For fear he'll go the self-same way.
I cannot once escape his eyes,
Whate'er he sees me do he tries.
Like me he says he's going to be
That little chap who follows me.
He knows that I am big and fine
And he believes in every word of mine.
The base in me he must not see
That little chap who follows me.
I must remember as I go
Through summer suns and winter snow.
I am building for the years to be
That little chap who follows me.

—Anonymous

The Four-Way Test is used as a guide for high ethical standards in athletics; it is used in plays and in preparing speeches and essays; it is used as the basis for presenting awards (to people who best live up to it); it is used in businesses, in the professions, in government and innumerable different ways throughout every walk and stratum of the world's society.

In Gifu, Japan, The Four-Way Test is engraved in bronze, on a monument erected to last a thousand years. But the important thing is: It is preserved in the hearts of countless people, uplifting their lives and bringing them closer to God. Psalm 24:1 says: "The earth is the Lord's and the fulness thereof; the world and they that dwell therein." We are trustees of the things God has placed in our hands, and we can all be better trustees if we

59

apply The Four-Way Test to everything we think, say, or do every day of our lives.

Daniel Webster, possibly America's greatest Secretary of State, was once asked to name the most profound thought he had ever had in his life. Quick as a flash, Mr. Webster replied: "My accountability to Almighty God." Daniel Webster knew he would have to account for the things God had placed in his trust—his time, his talents, his worldly goods, his thoughts, his affections and his physical body. The Four-Way Test helps all of us fulfill that job properly.

The Four-Way Test started in an office back in the days of the great depression—the result of a prayer for help to preserve the jobs of some 250 people and to save a bankrupt company.

Then, through the Christian Workers Foundation and Rotary International, it spread around the world and influenced the thoughts, words and actions of countless people and, through them, even governments and world events.

It is a test for all times and for all people. Yet, striking as its success and import have been, it has been equalled, perhaps, by miraculous progress in the other programs of the Christian Workers Foundation.

The spread of The Four-Way Test was only one part of God's plan for my life. So I trusted God, not knowing what the eventual result of these plans would be.

As usual, I was astounded—as you will see.

7

The Real Work Begins

It has always been my belief—that belief is supported by statistics—that crime always increases as ethical, moral and religious standards decline. The Near North Side of Chicago spawned its share of crime, but no more or less than other sections of other cities, towns and villages. It's not just a matter of poor living conditions and poverty, because great men have risen out of slums and ghettos. It is a matter, basically, of religious training—of guiding young people toward the eternal values of honesty, faith and high principles. The Near North Side was merely an example of this problem, that was constantly pressing in on me—a constant reminder that my work was only beginning. It was all well and good to sense the growing success of the Inter-Varsity Christian Fellowship, but there were other worlds to reach—the high-school student, the junior-high-school student, young people in the elementary grades and in preschool years.

Some years later, I remember reading words of J. Edgar Hoover, Director of the Federal Bureau of Investigation: "The criminal is the product of spiritual starvation. Someone failed miserably to bring him to know God, love Him and serve Him."

I knew this fact back in the days the Christian Workers Foundation was getting on its feet. The spiritual starvation of these young people related not only to their personal lives, but to the lives of all of us. The late John Foster Dulles put it this way once: "If we have failed to hold the respect of the world today, the answer to our problem is to go back to the beginning—to rediscover the spiritual basis to our society—for only individuals by their beliefs, conduct and example can make freedom a dynamic, persuasive thing. We must do this by remembering always the importance of moral, religious and spiritual values in our daily lives."

Here indeed was the challenge of the century—to reach out to millions of youngsters who were not being reached by the church and who received no spiritual food at home. As the Director of the Christian Workers Foundation, I knew we had few funds in those early days, but we did have faith and enthusiasm, and my wife and I saw the job that had to be done. With prayer and hard work, and with God's help in securing the right people, we knew we could use our resources wisely. We knew we could strike out at the heart of the major problem facing the country— the lack of spiritual and ethical training for millions of young people. Some of the religious powers took a rather narrow view of the Christian Workers Foundation. In those days, they didn't know who we were and they were suspicious of our desire to help make these organizations nondenominational. But we soon demonstrated the integrity of our efforts and God greatly blessed these projects in His service. Our *only* concern was the spiritual welfare of young people, and this objective was clearly in evidence from the beginning. It won us many friends even among the Christian leaders who had formerly been hesitant to commend our work. Probably you have not heard much about the Christian Workers Foundation. The reason is that God led us to establish a policy that did not seek publicity on our efforts or on the amount we contributed to these young people's projects, during their pioneering days. We knew the Bible said, ". . . let not thy left hand know what thy right hand doeth" (Matthew 6:3). The important thing was that God knew all about it.

After getting the United States' Inter-Varsity Christian Fellowship off to a sound start, we concentrated on a way to reach high-school students. Nothing came of the ideas we considered, until one day I had a talk with Ted Benson, a student at Dallas Theological Seminary, who had worked for the Christian Workers Foundation. I had been talking with him about our need to find a good way to reach the unchurched youngsters of high-school age.

Ted thought about it for a moment, then said, "Well, I know a young fellow at Dallas Theological Seminary—a junior—who has some ideas on the subject. However, his plans may seem a little strange when you first hear them."

The young man's name was James Rayburn and, a couple of days later, I decided to call him. I told him I'd pay his way up to Chicago, if he'd like to come and explain his "strange" ideas to me. He agreed and arrived on the appointed day. We sat down and discussed his program for reaching high-school students on a nondenominational basis. I remember telling him that day that maybe his ideas were the Lord's—maybe just his own—but, if he was willing to test them out, we would help him.

He thought about that, and then he said, "All right. At the end of this semester, I'd like to take a tent and set it up in Gainesville, Texas. I'll put my ideas to work and then give a full report at the end of the summer."

That sounded good to me, so I agreed to pay his expenses.

At the end of the summer, Jim and I had a long get-together. He had some success in Gainesville and had proved that his methods were sound. Essentially, his whole theory was to go out to unchurched, uninterested young people and *attract* them to Christ, rather than to *drive* them to Christ. Jim presented the gospel without long sermons. He did it with a fire and enthusiasm that appealed to young people, who might never, in a million years, step inside a church on their own. Jim's "strange" way of reaching these youngsters of high-school age was just what we needed.

Needless to say, I agreed, on behalf of the Christian Workers Foundation, to help him get started on a full-time basis. The

63

name of his organization is now well-known to almost everybody as "Young Life Campaign." The first Young Life Club was started in Dallas, Texas.

Young Life groups are now in more than forty states, and in 1967, Young Life had, in addition to scores of Young Life Clubs, more than 10,000 high-school-age youngsters attending its ranches in Colorado and in British Columbia in Canada.

Only one group that could reach high-school students didn't seem enough to me, though, so, when Young Life began moving along successfully, a second organization came to our attention. The right opportunity came along one day in the form of a good-looking, dedicated young man named Torrey Johnson. He walked into my office one day and said he wanted to hold some rallies for young people in downtown Chicago on Saturday nights. (At that time, Torrey was pastor of the Midwest Church on the North Side, and I knew a little bit about his work.) His idea seemed like a good one: He had already arranged to use a theater on Michigan Avenue, and what he needed was some organizational and financial help. He asked me to serve on the committee of the organization which was later called "Youth for Christ."

I served on the committee—and later on the Board for a number of years—and I was very impressed by the effectiveness of these rallies. My company had a program on the radio then, and when Torrey decided his messages should be on the air (and I agreed wholeheartedly with that) I arranged for the radio station to supply the time he needed.

Things went well for a while; then one day Torrey walked into my office with an unhappy look on his face, and said, "Well, it looks as if we're going to have to give up Youth for Christ. We owe $4,000 and we just don't have the money to pay it."

I knew the work he was doing was very effective and I told him: "There's no reason to give this work up. I'm sure you have at least ten people in Chicago who will give $200 each in order to keep Youth for Christ alive."

He said he thought that might be true.

"All right," I said, "you go to these people, and you tell them that you know a businessman who will donate $2,000 if ten of your own people donate $200 each."

About ten days went by and, sure enough, Torrey reappeared with the $2,000 he'd collected from interested people. I wrote out a check for the remaining $2,000 and Youth for Christ had a fresh start in Chicago.

There's little need to tell you how far Youth for Christ has progressed over the years. Surely, it is one of the world's most influential and positive forces for nondenominational evangelism among high-school-age young people. Besides helping Youth for Christ and Young Life emerge into the world and maintain their organizations on a sound footing, able to progress and reach tens of thousands of young people, we felt we had helped implement God's plan at the high-school-age level. Our next effort should be directed toward the *junior*-high-school level.

By this time I could see that God had a program to reach all ages of boys and girls. He had given me the privilege of seeing three of them reached by the gospel. What would come next? I was soon to learn.

Joe Coughlin was a student at Wheaton College, when I first heard about him in 1941. Friends of mine knew of my interest in organizations that were reaching the junior-high-school level and they mentioned Joe's name to me. He had organized two clubs: one called the "Christian Service Brigade"; the other—for girls —was called "Pioneer Girls." These groups met in churches, and Joe had organized them on a basis similar to that used in scouting. He made Christianity an interesting challenge for the young people and in addition to awards of the type given in scouting he gave awards for achievement in Christian progress. Somewhat like Jim Rayburn in his approach to young people, Joe made the attainment of Christian belief and principles an appealing adventure.

I asked Joe to come and talk with me, because I had heard

that his organization was considerably in debt. It was evident that Joe needed both financial assistance and guidance in managing business affairs.

After satisfying myself that Christian Service Brigade and Pioneer Girls were everything I had been led to believe, and after earnest praying about the situation, I knew that I had found the right man. Joe had the right methods to implement the plan of reaching unchurched young people at the junior-high-school level. I arranged for the Christian Workers Foundation to pay off his debts.

Just paying off debts, of course, was not a final solution, no more so than it had been for helping to finance the Young Life Campaign during its pioneering days. In all of these cases, the real need was for sound business management and good organization. God had given me many abilities and experiences in these directions and this instance was but another one where He led me to the right people and the right cause and said, in effect: "Here are the spiritual ideals and evangelical methods you need to implement My plan. Some of the important things needed to guarantee success are faith and the special talents I have given you."

Firmly believing that, I helped Joe organize a national board for Christian Service Brigade and also for Pioneer Girls. These organizations grew steadily from that point on. Today over 60,000 boys are in Christian Service Brigade and a larger number of girls are in Pioneer Girls. The rate of growth increases every year, and surveys show that fully half of the youngsters coming into these two fine organizations are led there by young people themselves. A majority of those who are being attracted into Christian Service Brigade and Pioneer Girls are unchurched youngsters who are brought into these Christian organizations by other Christian youngsters. Surely, there is no greater testimony to the effectiveness and farsightedness of Joe Coughlin's original ideas.

Still needed to complete the plan of reaching unchurched youth, was an organization for the elementary school level. This would include some preschool children as well, and the more I thought and prayed about this problem, the more difficult it seemed to solve. There just didn't seem to be any organization I could put my finger on that filled the need. When the Lord finally led me to the right solution, it came about in a surprising way.

The late Mrs. Phillip Armour—wife of an Armour & Company Meat Packers executive—was a member of our Inter-Varsity Christian Fellowship Board. Every time we held a meeting, somehow she managed to twist the conversation around and direct my thoughts toward a certain J. Irvin Overholtzer on the West Coast. Mr. Overholtzer had started some clubs on the West Coast specifically for the purpose of reaching the unchurched among the very young.

Finally, Mrs. Armour convinced me I should go to the West Coast and have a talk with Mr. Overholtzer. Child evangelism was close to my heart—it represented the one unfulfilled part of our God-given plan. When Mrs. Armour pointed out that what Mr. Overholtzer really needed was organizational ability, someone who could synchronize the work of his clubs on a national and international basis, the die was cast, and out I went.

As soon as I talked with Mr. Overholtzer, I knew that God had filled in the plan for me and, soon after my return to Chicago, we did what was necessary to organize "National Child Evangelism Fellowship," with Mr. Overholtzer's approval.

Child Evangelism Fellowship is a humble organization. You don't hear much about it, but in 1966, this organization reached over 900,000 children under eleven-years-old. People give sacrificially of their time and money to this marvelous organization and its operating system is a perfect example of how things should be done. All over the country, thousands of women and a limited number of dedicated men, form what is called "Good News Clubs." The children meet in homes, and most of these homes are close to elementary schools.

The women are trained to teach the Bible via the "flannel-graph" method, and recruiting for students is done outside of local schools. In some cases, cards are given to the youngsters as they leave school. The cards invite them to come to the Good News Club. More than 10,000 of these clubs meet every week in the United States, and most of the more than 900,000 young people, who were reached in parks, camps and vacation Bible schools, were unchurched. The youngsters came to the Good News Clubs and they learned about their heavenly ·Father, the gospel message of Christ, and the principles that can direct their lives into promising futures.

In addition to the Good News Clubs that function in the United States, the international division of the Child Evangelism Fellowship has more than 152 missionaries in over fifty foreign countries, who are setting up similar organizations to reach these very young people.

Child Evangelism Fellowship is the least publicized—certainly the least known—of the many groups the Lord has led me to aid. But, beyond a doubt, it is one of the most influential of all the organizations I've mentioned, in bringing children to a living knowledge of Jesus Christ.

About forty years ago, I memorized a short statement of Hudson Taylor, founder of the China Inland Mission. His words have been a great blessing to me over the years: "God's work, done in God's way, will never lack God's supply."

I have found Mr. Taylor's statement to be completely accurate especially in regard to winning cooperation and unanimous action, without which few things of importance can be accomplished as God would have them done.

Throughout the years, I have been chairman of twelve organizations—a total of 105 years as chairman. Never in this time has there been a negative vote on matters approved. By that, I mean that never has a motion or a plan of action failed to carry, eventually, by unanimous consent. In some early stages of negotiation, members of many boards opposed a proposed course of action. But, before final action was taken in the matter—through patience, logic, prayer and good humor—never has there been a motion that hasn't finally been adopted and carried by unanimous action.

The importance of winning cooperation cannot be overestimated, when the Lord's work is at stake. During the difficult days spent in helping to establish the six organizations I've just written about—days when we had to pioneer in new evangelical fields—unanimous agreement and action was a tremendous aid to progress.

It seems to me that proof that this work was directed by the Lord is seen in the wonderful cooperation of so many different people, with so many divergent views and opinions. Through it all, prayer was a daily routine for all of us. And, because we sought the same God, we were supplied with answers and strength by the same Holy Spirit, God's work was indeed carried on with unanimous consent and "never lacked supply." In the Bible, we find these words: "If any of you lack wisdom, let him ask of God, that giveth to all men liberally, and upbraideth not, and it shall be given him" (James 1:5). This passage gives us the answer to unanswered problems, which God wants solved.

Another thing I was continually aware of was that my work was never finished. I don't mean this begrudgingly—I loved almost every moment of my work, and I felt the challenge of helping to guide these organizations over the many obstacles they faced. But there were new kinds of challenges as well. It was becoming increasingly clear to me that the organizations we had helped, which were growing fast, would need many well-trained leaders to carry on their good work in the future. It was then that the Lord led us to begin developing Leadership Training Conference Grounds—I'll save that story for another chapter.

Right now, I'd like to tell you about one of the greatest forces for good that I know—Rotary!

8

Do unto Others . . .

THE PRINCIPAL reason for relating my experiences with the organizations mentioned in the last chapter is to emphasize again that God gave me a plan very early in life and, because I recognized it and trusted the Lord, all those things He planned for me have come to pass.

The point, and whole purpose of this book, is to prove that God has a plan for all of us, and anyone who will seek that plan with prayer and faith will find his whole life changed. It will become meaningful and charged with excitement and purpose. My case is just one illustration of this truth.

Another thing that helps immeasurably is to learn to recognize the things which are worthwhile—not only the basic values, such as integrity, honesty and faith—but organizations and groups which serve God and mankind without fanfare, but with great effectiveness. It is helpful to share the strength of these organizations, to learn from them and to know that strong forces for good are everywhere at work. Individuals can contribute to the organizations, and the organizations can contribute to the individual. Both grow stronger and infuse each other with an enthusiasm for good works and a comradeship that is not only a lasting source of inspiration, but a strong bulwark against slipping into a meaningless, unproductive life.

Among all the "nonreligious" organizations, surely the most outstanding and useful, in my opinion, is Rotary International.

I first joined Rotary in Paul's Valley. Soon after I came to Chicago I joined the Chicago Rotary Club and was its president from 1939 to 1940. In 1955, the fiftieth anniversary of the founding of Rotary, I served as president of Rotary International. Prior to 1955, I had served in almost every office in Chicago Rotary and had come to know thousands of Rotarians all over the world, particularly after The Four-Way Test had been adopted.

So—I know something about this wonderful organization, and I want to tell you a little story that I think best illustrates the true spirit of Rotary.

Several years ago, my wife Gloria and I were planning to go to Jerusalem. In those days, there was a fence in Jerusalem, and a traveler couldn't go from the Arab side of Jerusalem to the Israeli side. You had to fly to the island of Cyprus, get a visa, and then come back to the Israeli side.

Well, we were pondering the problem in a hotel in Ostend, when I saw two friends—both Rotarians—talking, over in a corner. I knew them both. One was a past president of the Tel Aviv Rotary Club, a Jew, and the other was a past president of the Beirut Rotary Club, an Arab. What do you think they were talking about?

They were trying to work out some way that Gloria and I could cross the boundary fence without having to fly to Cyprus to meet that nationalist regulation.

That was Rotary! No racial, religious or nationalistic roadblocks! Just two men trying to do something for somebody else. It was indeed a demonstration of the spirit of Rotary in its finest flower.

Today, Rotary International has over 600,000 business and professional men as members and more than 13,000 clubs in over 138 countries. The creed and spirit of Rotary continues to be: "Service above self."

71

Rotary not only erases nationalistic and other superficial barriers between men—its greatest contribution to world stability—it is, and has always been, active in directly supporting innumerable good causes. Rotary Clubs have adopted scores of poor villages and towns in many backward parts of the world, giving them hospitals, public sanitation, good roads and other needed improvements. Rotary has used its financial resources to aid flood victims, to establish scholarships, and to help millions of handicapped people all over the world. It would be almost impossible to list all of the charitable and philanthropic activities in which Rotary members are gladly involved, to say nothing of the civic functions carried out by Rotary—everything from helping to straighten out young criminals to raising funds for a local firehouse. My definition of Rotary is as follows: Rotary is a maker of friendships, a builder of men and communities and a creator of goodwill and friendship between the peoples of the world.

The late Sir Winston Churchill, himself an honorary member of Rotary, said of this international organization that it exerts a powerful influence for moral and spiritual values. Like sentiments have been expressed by President Dwight D. Eisenhower, by Chiang Kai-Shek and by most of the free world's leading statesmen. More than a third of the members of the U.S. Senate are members of Rotary.

All of these words just scratch the surface, when it comes to telling you about Rotary. A history of Rotary, "The Golden Strand," has been published by Quandrangle Press in Chicago. It contains more than 300 information-packed pages about an organization every American should know more about.

Possibly the most important thing that Rotary does is build better citizens. In 1940, when I was president of Chicago Rotary, I gave a little talk to the members and part of it went like this:

I believe that the great opportunity and the great responsibility of Rotary rests in the field of building character, in

72

the building of men. In fact, I think this is the great task of all Rotary Clubs, building men who will be available for service in the various walks of life; in politics, in business, in community affairs, and in their homes as fathers and husbands. There is such a great need for good citizenship and leadership. There are many fields in which the real leader is welcome—and needed. There is the problem of corruption and waste in local government. There is the problem of strife between employer and employee. There is the problem of crime in the streets. There is the problem of securing international peace and understanding.

But I think the greatest opportunity for Rotary is in developing leaders who will take their religious faith, and the ideals that come from it, and put them into practice in everyday life, in the home, in business and in community activities. If we take the ideals of truth, justice and love of our fellow men, and put them into constant practice, Rotarians can work wonders. And this means that Rotary can work wonders because the measure of Rotary lies in the life of the average Rotarian. It is the way of life he leads and the way he treats his fellow men.

It isn't every gathering of business and professional men where a man can stand up, say the things I just did, and find general acceptance and agreement. That, however, is the spirit of Rotary.

I am convinced, beyond any doubt, that part of God's plan for my life is my association with Rotary, because in addition to having furthered my opportunity to be usefully involved in local, national and international affairs, it gives me an opportunity to talk about it and to direct your attention toward this unique organization. If you are ever invited to a Rotary International luncheon, and you ask for the butter, and it is handed down the table to you, first by a Japanese, then by a Nigerian, then by a Frenchman and finally by a businessman from Arkan-

73

sas—all of them smiling during the process and passing pleasantries with each other—you'll witness the finest kind of brotherhood in action. All of these men are setting examples that any man would be wise to follow.

Rotarians are trying to do unto others as they would want others to do unto them—the kind of inspiration of which the world needs a lot more.

Rotary—or a Rotary member, such as myself—may possibly play a role in God's plan for your own life.

Whoever he is, he'll be worth listening to.

9

Preparing for the Future

JIM RAYBURN, you'll remember, was the young man who started Young Life, in a tent in Gainesville, Texas. Well, he called me one afternoon and, in his usual effervescent way, said that he wanted Young Life to buy a ranch in Colorado Springs. Would I be willing to come out to see the ranch, he asked. He wanted to use it as a conference ground where high-school young people could come, learn about Christ in a pleasant atmosphere, and be trained for future leadership in Young Life.

I told Jim to calm down—that my wife Gloria and I would fly out, have a look at the ranch, and have a talk with him about it.

Young Life had been going along very well and had attracted many hundreds of youngsters. Jim's idea of a conference training ground was really in line with my own thoughts for *all* the organizations I'd helped to sponsor—we would be needing future leaders—but I didn't want to rush into this matter.

It was about twenty-two years ago that Gloria and I flew out to see the ranch at Colorado Springs. Jim was about thirty-three years old then, but he acted like a teen-ager. He couldn't wait for us to see the ranch—Star Ranch, it was called, a former gambling spa. I wish you could have been there! The ranch was absolutely beautiful, nestled in among the foothills of the Cheyenne Mountains, and we were overawed by the magnificent scenery. Up to now, Young Life had been renting camps wherever they could find them on a pretty much hit-and-miss basis.

75

There was no central conference ground where young people could relax and really get the full benefit of Jim's unique teaching systems. The worst part of it was that the youngsters would come to a camp meeting and then, after the camp period ended, we might never see many of them again. It wasn't a good situation at all, as Jim pointed out to us many times while we were in Colorado Springs.

"This is what we need," Jim said, breathlessly. "Mountains, and fresh air and open country—a place where young people will *want* to come. And all it costs is $50,000!"

To make a long story short, my wife and I were convinced that Young Life should buy Star Ranch. At that time I was Chairman of the Board of Trustees, and when we returned to Chicago we called the members of the Young Life Board together. The Board had a few doubts about the project. Jim loved mountain climbing, and some of the members figured that was one of the reasons he really wanted the ranch. There might have been some truth in that, but I knew that Jim's overriding motivation was to help young people, and I had seen that demonstrated many times. I felt that the Holy Spirit convinced Jim at that time that we should have Star Ranch. The real problem, however, was the Board members were not wealthy people, and $50,000 was just too much money to raise. They also had some doubts about young people being willing to go out to Colorado Springs.

After prayer about the matter I was convinced that God wanted Young Life to have Star Ranch. Miraculously, I managed to raise the money through the Christian Workers Foundation and we bought Star Ranch for Young Life.

The first group of unchurched youngsters to "christen" Star Ranch was a rowdy gang from Colorado Springs High School. Jim, with the help of friends, had managed to find just one lone Christian at the high school—"Fuzz" Cunning—and Fuzz managed to drag fifty students to the ranch for a long weekend.

This was the sort of atmosphere, of course, in which Jim worked best. The tougher and rougher the kids, the more challenging they were, the better Jim operated. He'd rubbed elbows with some of the worst delinquents and tough guys in the United States, and if this particular bunch expected to faze Jim, they were wrong.

So wrong, in fact, that after about a year, three hundred young people were coming to Young Life Club meetings from that one high school alone!

Even Young Life leaders have been amazed at the immense progress Star Ranch has made. Week after week, hundreds of young people lose their prejudices in the beautiful surroundings at Star Ranch. They respond to the Word of God and return to their homes and schools to witness for their new-found Saviour.

As Star Ranch outgrew itself, other ranches were added. Silver Cliff Ranch was the first, and boasted the hottest natural spring in Colorado. Then, in 1951, a magnificent piece of property was purchased on Mt. Princeton by fourteen friends of Young Life for over $225,000 and turned over to the group. It is now known as Frontier Ranch.

During its first twenty years, more than 1,000 young people came to Star Ranch, alone, each year. Jim Rayburn is retired now, but I asked him recently how many young people he really thought became Christians while they were at Star Ranch.

Jim thought a moment, then he said: "Herb, at the very least —the very least—no less than one-half of them."

Now, that figures out to be at least 10,000 youngsters. And that's just the blessings from *one* of Young Life's four ranches.

As a matter of fact, Young Life's accomplishments were so dramatic and so obvious to everybody, that Inter-Varsity Christian Fellowship and the Navigators—another organization we've aided through the Christian Workers Foundation—bought their own ranches in the Rocky Mountains. There are now five wonderful Christian ranches in Colorado.

And all of it began with Jim Rayburn—a fellow who had a plan and the Lord's leading to attract young people to Christianity with some methods that many people in the early days thought were "strange."

As we saw how the Lord was starting to bless us so much with Star Ranch, we turned our attention toward establishing leadership training conference grounds for the other groups we'd helped organize. As usual, I couldn't predict with certainty where the Lord was going to lead us, and, also as usual, there were a few surprises in store.

I knew about a particularly beautiful tract of land on Prentiss Bay in the resort area of northern Michigan. It seemed just what we needed for Inter-Varsity Christian Fellowship. Of all of our organizations, IVCF would be in need of new leaders soonest, and we very much wanted to establish a conference training ground for them as quickly as possible.

The tract of land we were interested in had been owned by a lumberman. He had died and left the property to nine heirs. The heirs were scattered all over the country—New Jersey, Michigan, and one heir who lived in the East was a minor (under twenty-one years of age).

Finding it difficult to get the heirs together to agree to sell the land, and to set a price, I assigned Kenneth Hansen, a young man who was then working for the Christian Workers Foundation, to go and see all these people, explain our need for the land, and get them to agree to sell at a fair price. After working on the project for over two years, Ken managed to get seven of the nine heirs to go along with us. The remaining two heirs were elderly ladies who actually spent their summers on the property at Prentiss Bay. They lived in a cottage up there and had built a second one, which they rented out. Ken had not been able to convince them, and the time came that I thought maybe I should have a try at them.

It wasn't the resort season yet, so the ladies hadn't gone up to Prentiss Bay. They had another home on the edge of Cheboygan, Michigan, and that's where I found them. When I arrived, they were sitting on the porch, knitting.

I introduced myself, told them about our efforts to purchase the land and the agreements we'd reached with the other heirs.

Then I explained carefully just what we wanted to do with the land: It would be used to build Christian character, to train college-age people to go into foreign missionary fields and to be the leaders of IVCF on college campuses in the future.

Well, after two hours of talking, I hadn't made a dent—and I was supposed to be a salesman!

As I turned to leave, I whispered a short prayer. I said, "Lord, if you want this land for Inter-Varsity, please tell me what to do." I hadn't walked ten feet when I felt compelled to turn around and speak once more to the two ladies. This is what I said: "I've got a last word for you, and I think this comes directly from the Lord. I wouldn't want to be in your shoes on the Judgement Day."

I walked on, but before I'd gone another fifteen feet, one of the ladies shouted for me to return. I came back and they asked me to wait a few minutes while they went inside for a discussion. In a short while they came out—they signed up!

In a sense, it could be said that I actually had to frighten these two women to get them to agree to sell their Prentiss Bay property—but that was the way the Lord led me in answer to my prayer.

Swiftly after that, the tract on Prentiss Bay began to be transformed from a two-cottage resort to a wonderful, full-of-life conference grounds for dedicated young college students whose central thought in life was to serve their Lord.

After the Christian Workers Foundation purchased the property for IVCF, the Foundation also built the first lodge—a beautiful building that seats 200 people in the dining room, 200 in the meeting room, and accommodates more than 80 girls in the upstairs dormitories. There are big picture windows on all sides of the lodge, and the view of Prentiss Bay is truly spectacular.

I've always believed that the Lord wanted sound, practical construction and beauty in the many buildings we've helped build on our conference grounds—it doesn't seem likely that He would want it any other way, does it? A perfect example of this is the main building at Star Ranch in Colorado, which is made of the finest stone and is topped by a magnificent tile roof.

The lodge at Cedar Campus—which is what we named the property at Prentiss Bay—was also constructed of the best materials available and cost about $65,000. This was back in the early 1950's, when $65,000 bought a lot more than it does today, but even so we had a hard time coming up with the final $10,000. The Christian Workers Foundation didn't have it at that time, and it looked as if we would have to save on the cost of the lodge by eliminating the eaves, which would have seriously impaired the beauty of the building.

Well, the Lord stepped in again, because that year—1954-1955—I was President of Rotary International, and do you know what they give their presidents as an honorarium?

Right. $10,000.

So, I just asked them to make the check out to the Christian Camps Foundation—a special nonprofit corporation set up to provide money for our conference grounds projects in Michigan. We got our beautiful lodge, *with* eaves!

The help provided by other foundations must be mentioned here also—notably the Kresge Foundation in Detroit, which contributed importantly to all six of the evangelical organizations with which I was connected; the Crowell Foundation in Chicago, established by the former Chairman of the Board of the Quaker Oats Company, contributed to five of the organizations.

So, from every quarter there was help and enthusiasm for the training camp projects, and my next obvious step was to help establish one for The Christian Service Brigade.

As usual, we had to overcome some strange obstacles.

About twenty-five years ago, before I'd ever heard about Joe Coughlin and his Christian Service Brigade, I made one of my infrequent visits back to the family home in Pickford, Michigan. My brother had taken over the lumber business from my father, and we got to reminiscing this particular day about Rapsom Creek

—a beautiful stretch of trout stream that I had fished as a boy.

As we talked about the great fun and adventure we used to have along Rapsom Creek, I turned to my brother Harold impulsively and said, "You know, I'd like to buy Rapsom Creek. I have an idea it would make a wonderful boy's camp someday."

Startled, my brother turned to me and said, "Why, you can't buy Rapsom Creek! Scores of people own that creek—it's four miles long!"

Well, I had it in my mind to buy Rapsom Creek for a boy's camp—which shows how far in advance the Lord was leading me—because this was many, many years before I became involved in establishing leadership training camps. I had no idea what *kind* of a boy's camp I wanted to establish eventually, except that it would be a Christian boy's camp.

I set aside my brother's objections and got on with my plan: "We can't have a boy's camp, unless we own the whole creek. You know that. We can't have a boy's camp without good trout fishing, and we can't have good fishing unless we own the entire creek and the land around it, so we can post it to keep other people off."

Then I asked Harold to get a tax map, find out who owned the land along Rapsom Creek, and to start buying it up at a per-acre price I had arrived at.

Sixteen years later—that's how long it took us to acquire all the land parcels—we owned the whole of Rapsom Creek and over 1,800 surrounding acres of northern woods, wild game and trails.

Our next project was to build a lake and to put in electrical power and roads. I still didn't know definitely what the eventual outcome would be, but the lake was finally finished—over half-a-mile long and a third-of-a mile wide—and the total investment at that point was about $48,000.

That's how things stood until 1958. We had this beautiful spot for a perfect boy's camp, but it wasn't until 1958 that the Lord made plain to me what we should do with it.

Since turning the camp over to the Christian Service Brigade, buildings and other improvements have been added to the Rapsom Creek property, of course, and we even have a 2200-foot airstrip where some of the boys learn to fly, for eventual missionary service in remote regions of the world. There is a great need for pilot-missionaries and the Brigade camp in Pickford, called "Northwoods", is helping to provide them.

The teen-agers who go to Northwoods are trained to be Christian leaders, not only to serve the Christian Service Brigade in the future, but to serve in many places, in many ways throughout the world. One man put it nicely, when he said: "The dollars invested in Northwoods do not only represent an investment in property; they have been invested in young manhood. The funds will be paying dividends through eternity. Who knows what the Lord will do with one teen-ager challenged to selfless Christian leadership? A teen today could become another Jonathan Edwards, D. L. Moody, or Apostle Paul and 'turn the world upside down'!"

Northwoods represents the clearest example in my life of how the Lord had directed my steps from the beginning. And every time I contemplate his miraculous guidance in regard to Northwoods, I can't help but recall my brother's excited words: "Why, you can't buy Rapsom Creek! It's four miles long!"

Harold just didn't know he was competing with God's plan!

In this chapter, I've been concerned with how we started the first leadership training camps for the evangelical organizations we had concentrated on helping during the early days of the Christian Workers Foundation. These training camps represented the second part of the overall job that had to be done—making sure that responsible Christian leaders would be available in the future to carry on the work of these five evangelical youth groups.

Of course, many more camps came along, and there were many regional camps and various training divisions. We bought an attractive property for a leadership training camp for Pioneer

Girls, just across the Bay from Cedar Campus. And this camp has been just about as successful and meaningful as all the others. It would take too much space and time to give a detailed account of all our activities in this field, which currently include helping to build a model children's camp for Child Evangelism, but there is a particularly interesting story in connection with our work with the Lifeline Division of Youth for Christ, that I'd like to tell you about.

You'll remember how highly I rated Rotary as a force for moral and ethical good. Well, I'd been asked to speak to Rotarians and Kiwanis—another fine organization—and later I was to speak in Fredericksburg, Virginia, at the annual meeting of the Chamber of Commerce. I turn down many such invitations, but something led me to pray about this particular request. After praying, I didn't have a really strong feeling that I was being led to make the trip, but a little "something" urged me to go. Not fully understanding, but not wanting to turn my back on what might be the Lord's leading, I went down to Fredericksburg.

While I was there, some of the men told me about George Washington's former home. About a mile outside of Fredericksburg, Ferry Farm was the place George Washington lived from the time he was six until he was twenty-two. He chopped down the cherry tree in that yard; threw the silver dollar across the Rappahannock River that borders the property. Both his mother and father died on the property and a reproduction of George Washington's little surveyor's hut stands next to the house, where it was originally.

I learned that a nonprofit organization, composed of thirty business and professional men in Fredericksburg, owned the home and lands, and they operated it as a memorial to George Washington. They even had a museum on the grounds and charged fifty cents admission. The entire property comprised about 100 acres and, because funds were in short supply, the museum and other aspects of the memorial were somewhat rundown.

I became so interested in Ferry Farm I decided to run out and have a look. One look convinced me that here, again, was a perfect site for a character-building project for young people. What youngster could help but benefit immeasurably from being exposed, over a long period of time, to the very place where the Father of Our Country grew up, matured and learned the values that shaped him into the great man he became?

I did some serious thinking the rest of the day, and I prayed for direction, because there was no doubt in my mind now that the Lord had directed my steps to Fredericksburg and, via Rotarians and Kiwanis, had presented me with an opportunity to serve Him again. After a while I found my thoughts directed clearly toward the Lifeline Division of Youth for Christ.

Youth for Christ has about sixty camps, throughout the United States, that take in juvenile boys. The boys come from the courts and juvenile judges, and they are allowed to go to a Lifeline camp for one week. During this one week of camping, some of the boys become Christians. A lot of them have no homes and no family at all, and all of us connected with Youth for Christ are continually concerned about these youngsters—especially those who become Christians at camp and then have nowhere to go.

As I pondered this problem in Fredericksburg, it seemed to me that the Lord had given me at least one good answer to this problem in the form of the spacious 100-acre, George Washington Memorial Home and grounds.

Becoming convinced of it, I asked who was responsible for the actual operation of the memorial, and when they told me it was an Executive Committee, I told them I'd stay overnight if they would call the committee into meeting the following day.

The meeting was arranged, and the next day I presented my plan to the committee. They agreed to sell the property to Youth for Christ to use as a camp for underprivileged boys. It was one of the happiest transactions of my career, and I thank the Lord continually for seeing to it I went to Fredericksburg despite my doubts.

Today, the new, beautiful George Washington Memorial Home houses fifteen boys. They're going to school where George Washington went to school; they're learning, working and playing in a wonderful, inspiring atmosphere. Eventually, we plan to house at least 100 boys at the Home and new buildings are being planned to accomplish this objective. A house mother and a house father are always in residence at the Home.

As an illustration of the kind of young men living at the Home: The first nine boys who came didn't receive a single letter during a sixty-day period. The boys at the George Washington Memorial Home are selected very carefully. They are ex-juvenile delinquents who become Christians, and who have fine talents worth developing and they have no homes of their own.

Our future plans include helping the boys to obtain scholarships to colleges, and we hope to guide them into careers of their own choosing. We expect a substantial number will go into the Lord's work and be in the forefront of those who, in future years, will help to lead other delinquents into useful lives.

Everything the Christian Workers Foundation was connected with during all these years can appropriately be called pioneering. We cut new trails, tried new ideas, experimented with new systems and methods. All was done in league with God's constant and neverfailing help and guidance. The need, the people and ideas to answer the need, and the funds and organizational talents were supplied by the Lord—often miraculously—and have resulted in God's work being done. One of the great blessings that has come to me in recent years is to have my very dear friend Robert Walker, together with my two fine, Christian sons-in-law, Allen W. Mathis, Jr. and G. Robert Lockhart, become members of the Board of Trustees of Christian Workers Foundation.

At times, the Lord led us to pioneer in other areas.

For example, there was the Billy Graham Crusade in Chicago in 1962—the Crusade that almost didn't materialize. . . .

85

10

A Miracle and a Crusade

WHENEVER I THINK about Billy Graham—and that is quite often, because he is a good friend and an outstanding servant of the Lord's—I almost always relate it to two events in my life: his Chicago Crusade in 1962, and his interest in the fact that I memorized the Sermon on the Mount and repeat it to myself every day.

There is an interesting story behind each of these events, and the facts that lead up to my memorizing of the Sermon on the Mount I believe constitute a miracle.

Dr. Charles E. Fuller's radio program, the "Old-fashioned Revival Hour," is known and remembered by many thousands—perhaps millions—of people. But, in its early days in 1939, this great preaching was heard by only a few people because Dr. Fuller didn't have enough money at the same time both to advertise and to put his program on more stations.

I heard about the problem and arranged to donate some funds for advertising purposes for about two years. At the end of this time, the situation had improved, and Dr. Fuller was able to support his very worthy activities with incoming funds from other sources.

For me, the important part of my contribution was that it enabled me to come to know and love Dr. Fuller. He became a close family friend.

In 1947, I was ill with an "unknown" fever. I kept getting weaker and weaker, until I was confined to bed in my home. The doctors had no idea what was wrong with me. Even specialists couldn't diagnose my illness. I was really very ill, and there seemed to be a good chance I might not recover. I remember thinking how well God's plan had been working out in my life— several evangelical youth organizations were now on their feet and were reaching out effectively for millions of young people— and I couldn't quite believe that God was going to let it end here. I was already aware of the great need for leadership training camps, and I knew there was a lot of work still to be done.

And here I lay, so sick I couldn't get out of bed!

One afternoon, the door of my room opened and in walked Dr. Fuller. He'd just flown in from California, and he wanted to talk with me about founding an evangelical seminary. He asked about my health, but he didn't seem deeply disturbed about it. It was as if he considered my illness strictly a temporary problem.

We talked for a while about the need for a seminary to train future Christian leaders, not only for the many youth organizations I was a part of, but for churches and missionary projects around the world. I agreed with the need and told him I'd help him get the seminary underway.

With that taken care of, Dr. Fuller started to leave. As he stood up, he turned to me and said, "I need your help, you know. So I'm going to pray that you get well."

It was just as casual as that. But he said it like a man who knew exactly what the tremendous power of prayer can be, from a man who seeks God's will and prays in accord with that will.

The very next day, the doctors discovered I had undulant fever, which must have been contracted from drinking unpasteurized milk—undulant fever is a rare illness and the last thing anyone had suspected. (It was later determined that I had contracted the disease twenty-four years before when I had drunk unpasteurized milk, in Paul's Valley, Oklahoma.)

It took several months to convalesce, and hardly a day of that time passed that I did not reflect upon the miracle of Dr. Fuller's visit, that his prayer in my behalf had been answered.

Today, I am a trustee of Fuller Seminary, and it is a blessed association. During the past twenty-one years, Fuller Seminary has provided our Lord with about 1,000 splendid young men who have a deep faith in the Bible and who have spread the gospel message of Christ to many remote corners of the earth. In 1966, alone, Young Life had fifteen Fuller graduates on its staff, and thirteen Fuller alumni were on the staff of Inter-Varsity Christian Fellowship.

Dr. Fuller's prayer for me was answered. In turn, my prayer for many trained, responsible Christian leaders was answered.

During the weeks of convalescence that followed the diagnosis of my illness, I happened across these words of Christ's in John 14:21: "He that hath my commandments, and keepeth them, he it is that loveth me."

The word "hath" carried a lot of meaning for me, because to have Christ's commandments truly doesn't mean that we just read them once in a while, but that we know them by heart and *have* them in our hearts. Realizing this, I asked the Lord to direct me to the commandments Christ had for me. I was led to Matthew 5, 6, and 7—the Sermon on the Mount.

It took me about a month to memorize those three chapters, but I finally accomplished it and I have repeated them to myself every single day of my life ever since; and I will continue to repeat them.

Sometimes, I'm asked how I find time to repeat a number of chapters of Scripture to myself each day, because I've memorized many other passages, in addition to the Sermon on the Mount. People are startled by the great amount of work I have to do, and they can't understand how I can take the time to strengthen my faith each day by setting aside a definite amount of time for prayer, the reading of God's word and repeating from memory the life-giving Scriptures of God's Word.

Paul wrote that faith comes by hearing the Word of God, and

88

Christ tells us that if a man gains the world, but loses his soul, he has made a mighty poor bargain. Now, the soul is saved through faith, and if faith comes by hearing the Word of God, then what a foolish predicament a man is in if he doesn't consult his Bible on a regular basis!

I spend about an hour and fifteen minutes a day reading, memorizing and repeating the Scripture from memory. That's less than some people take for lunch! It's less time than most of us take for our three meals a day!

Spiritual food, which comes from a regular diet of God's Word, is the most meaningful and important food we can give our souls. I challenge—and I'll repeat it—I *challenge* anyone to read Christ's Sermon on the Mount, and then—after thinking about it carefully—to put it down without knowing in his heart that here indeed, in these beautiful words, is the formula for peace, for brotherhood, and for all of the fine things for which men have yearned since the dawn of creation.

The next step is to practice the precepts given in the Sermon on the Mount. By doing so, a man will know that he is closer to God and that he is making a God-directed contribution toward mankind and the world we live in. He will feel better. He will go farther. He will accomplish more. He will overcome self-doubts and fears. He will gain confidence. And, in the end, he will inherit the eternal promises made to every man who holds firmly to the faith that Jesus is the Christ.

Billy Graham wrote me and said that he has told the story of my daily repetition, from memory, of the Sermon on the Mount, to people all over the world; and that when folk hear it, they are moved to follow the Lord.

If you'd like to find out, try reading Matthew 5, 6, and 7. In just the few minutes you spend on those chapters, you may have the first glimpse of God's plan for *your* life.

My major association with Billy Graham occurred in 1962. I was Chairman of the Executive Committee for Billy Graham's

Greater Chicago Crusade, and the events leading up to this Crusade are no less miraculous than those that resulted in the diagnosing and curing of my undulant fever. They illustrated again the eternal truth in Hudson Taylor's statement that God's work, done in God's way, will never lack God's supply.

Several years prior to 1962, I'd talked with Billy Graham about having a Crusade in Chicago. He wasn't very much in favor of it. As a matter of record, he was solidly against it, and he had some good reasons. He began by quoting Christ's words about a prophet not having honor in his own country. Then he explained that he had graduated from nearby Wheaton College; that his first church had been in Chicago; that his first job with Youth for Christ had been in Chicago; and that the Chicago Federation of Churches had not seen fit to invite him to hold a Crusade in that city. Then he said something that, in the light of all these facts, was not too surprising: "I don't think I will ever have a Crusade in Chicago."

I was disheartened to hear this, so I said to Billy: "Well, all of this may be so, but you don't mind if a few of us pray about it, do you?"

He said, "No," and although I believe he didn't feel anything would come of it, I was also positive that if prayers should clearly reveal God's wish for him to come to Chicago with a Crusade, he would do it. Billy Graham's only concern was that it might not be God's will. If it proved to be otherwise, no force on earth would keep that great man of God from preaching in our city.

As we parted that afternoon, a plan was already forming in my mind. Chicago I felt, of all cities, needed a Billy Graham Crusade, and I prayed long and earnestly for God to help me, if my convictions about Chicago and Billy Graham were right. I knew nothing would come of it, if I were wrong.

As a first step I was led to carefully select eleven responsible laymen from eleven denominations other than my own (Methodist). The Church Federation had not invited Billy to

90

come to Chicago, so I felt I had to start with the laymen. The men I selected were leaders in their denominations. We formed a committee and began to pray and to lay our plans. Billy even met with us once and repeated his doubts that God wanted him to hold a Crusade in Chicago.

Regardless of the lack of encouragement from Billy, which is an inspiring testimony to his commitment to God's will, our committee went out and got over 300 laymen—each one carefully chosen—to agree to a statement of faith and that they thought it would be a wonderful thing for the spiritual life of Chicago if Billy Graham were to hold a Crusade in our city.

Then we asked the 300 laymen to invite their ministers—and as many ministers in Chicago as they could influence—to come to a breakfast meeting at the Conrad Hilton Hotel. We promised we'd have Billy Graham there as the speaker.

On the morning of the breakfast over 700 ministers and about 300 laymen filed into the room—more than a thousand people. It was an inspiring sight. We had done our best to arrange for at least one layman to be at each of the tables, and, when everything settled down, Billy stood up and brought an inspiring message on the great need for a spiritual awakening in Chicago.

When he finished, I offered a strong invitation to Billy to come to Chicago and hold a Crusade. I looked over the audience and spoke directly to the laymen first. I said, "How many of you think it would be a wonderful thing for the spiritual life of Chicago if Billy Graham came here with a Crusade? Will you please stand up?"

Every layman in the room, as far as I could tell, immediately stood up.

Then I said, "Is there any layman here who doesn't think it would be a good thing for the spiritual life of Chicago for Billy Graham to hold a Crusade? Please stand up."

Not a man left his chair. The room was absolutely silent.

Then I turned to the ministers, and I said: "Now you've seen how your leading laymen feel. I'd like to get an indication of how *you* feel about it. Will the ministers who believe a Billy Graham crusade would be a wonderful thing for the spiritual life of Chicago please stand up?"

I looked around the room, and apparently every minister was standing up! To make sure, I asked them to sit down and I rephrased the question: "Will the ministers who do *not* think so please stand up?"

No one stood up.

Then I turned to Billy and I said, "Billy, here you have over 700 ministers and 300 leading laymen, who have given you a unanimous invitation to come to Chicago and hold a Crusade."

Billy got up and said: "I will, as soon as possible, hold a meeting of our team, and I will send you a telegram giving their decision.

About two weeks later, we got a telegram saying he'd come and hold a Crusade in Chicago!

When we received that telegram, most of us who had worked so hard on the project knew, with a certainty, that whatever God wants to have done, can be done. He only needs the people to do it, and we breathed a prayer of thanks that He had seen fit to entrust us with the pioneering of this particular mission.

Billy held his Greater Chicago Crusade in McCormick Place in June of 1962. Over 3000 churches cooperated in conducting the Crusade. God blessed the Crusade in a mighty way and many Crusade records were broken, including the largest average daily attendance at any Crusade in America up to that time; the largest single crowd—116,000 on the last day of the Crusade at Soldier's Field—and the average contribution per person attending the Crusade was about one third greater than at previous crusades. Total money raised by the Crusade was about $719,000. Over and above all expenses, we were able to provide over $186,000 to the Billy Graham Evangelistic Association to help pay for television replays of the Crusade on something like 180 stations in the United States, Canada, Australia and

New Zealand. Approximately 17,000 came forward to the counseling rooms after Billy gave the invitations. A large majority of these became new, born-again Christians.

From almost every standpoint, Billy Graham's Greater Chicago Crusade in 1962 was a great success. A press release right after the Crusade, said: "We thank God for this Crusade for Christ has greatly changed the complexion of Chicago by diverting our words, thoughts and deeds from material and temporal values to moral, ethical, spiritual and eternal things."

Billy Graham commented: "We all agree that people everywhere in Chicago discussed religion during the crusade, and I believe some churches here feel a real spiritual awakening."

11

Time, Talents
and Friends

YEARS AGO, when I attended Northwestern University, there
were four things pulling on me for my time.

First, I had to work my way through college. I had two sisters
in college at the same time I was at Northwestern, and my father
did not have enough money to take care of my expenses. That
meant I had to earn my way as I went. That took time.

Second, obviously I had to use some of my time for my studies. I wanted to get good grades and to secure something of
permanent value out of the courses I was taking.

Third, I knew it would be a good idea to get some experience
in extra-curricular activities that would be of help to me after I
finished college. And that took some time.

And fourth, during the beginning of my sophomore year, I fell
deeply in love with a beautiful high-school sophomore. There
were seven other fellows trying their best to get this girl, so you
can be sure this took some of my time, too. Here's an illustration
of what I used to do to make the best possible use of my time.

During my sophomore year, I was running the half-mile and
the mile on the Northwestern University track team. We had a
track meeting coming up with the Chicago Athletic Association.
I was holding down two jobs also: one as sportswriter for two
Chicago newspapers, the other as a telegraph operator for Western Union. I would send in my reports directly from the gym or

the stadium to the newspapers, and this meant they got on the street a little earlier than competing papers.

On the day of this particular track meet, after arranging to telegraph it for Western Union, I asked for, and got, a date with my girl friend. Then I took the elevated railway down to Rogers Park to get her. The trip took about twenty-five minutes, so I took my textbook along and did some studying. Of course, I didn't do any studying while I was riding back with her on the elevated. When we got back to the gymnasium, I took my girl friend—the then Gloria Forbrich—up into the press box overlooking the stands, excused myself, went down and put on my track suit and robe. Then I came back up, and sent in a lead story giving details about the meet and some statistics and brief biographical sketches of the athletes.

When the mile was called, I excused myself again, went down to the track and ran the mile. Then I came up and reported the mile. A little later, when the half-mile was called, I again made my apologies to Gloria, scooted down to the track and ran the half-mile. Then I came back up and reported the half-mile.

When the meet was finished, I sent in the final story to the newspapers and took Gloria home.

In this way, I found time for all four things that night. I earned something like $16.00 for the newspaper reporting and for the telegraphing; I had a date with my girl friend and kept her away from those seven other fellows; I ran the half-mile and the mile and even did some studying on the elevated train!

I suppose I might add that I didn't win the mile or the half-mile, but I did eventually win the girl.

That is an example of what I think about time. It is a good idea to use it wisely. Sir Walter Scott wrote a poem about time:

Before my breath, like blazing flax,
Man and his marvels pass away.
And changing empires wane and wax,
Are founded, flourish and decay.

It constantly amazes me that so many people think so little of time, one of life's most valuable possessions, given to every man in equal amounts every day, until it is stopped by death. Of all things given to men, time is the most temporal. It must be used well while it is available, if it is to be of any advantage at all. And, if it is used well—if every minute is invested in the future —time is no longer temporal, and passing, nor is it denied to you when you die. It becomes eternal. That's the secret and the promise of using time wisely.

If a man invests money wisely and early, he may well reach a point in life where he does not need to earn another nickel, but is able to live comfortably from the income he receives on his investments.

The same thing applies to time. If a person considers time carefully and asks himself what it really is, he will *invest* it so he doesn't run out of it. However, he will first have to come to some important conclusions, as this little phrase points out so well: "Only one life, t'will soon be past; only that done for Christ will last."

The man who invests a part of his money carefully, knows that if he does not, he will run out of it someday and will be in trouble. The man who invests a part of his time carefully, by seeking to understand God and His will and by determining God's plan for his life, will be given an eternity of time, when his earthly allotment has expired. There is certainly no better investment.

Sir Wilfred Grenfell was a young doctor who might have captured international acclaim had he chosen to invest his time for his own material advancement. But early in his life, he caught a vision of a life served for Christ and for others. He gave everything up to labor in cold, barren, cheerless Labrador in order to bring new life and hope to that forgotten corner of the world. Grenfell's story is not unlike that of many other men who have sensed the true value of time and *invested* it, rather than *spent* it.

The man who tells you, "I never had a chance!" and goes on

reading his pin-up magazine or sprawls for hours in front of his television set, is waiting for that vague "break" that will never come. He is wasting a precious commodity, and that "chance" he says he never had is the same "chance" given to all of us. It is called time, and every single one of us has no more or less of it in the course of a day than anyone else. So—he has little excuse for his attitude. He dooms himself with it as surely as if he had no time given to him at all. Every moment of our lives is an opportunity to learn and to invest in the future.

To get the most from a twenty-four-hour day—I'm talking about examples that have been set by most of the successful men I know—it is necessary to regulate habits. A good way to do so is to make up a complete time budget for the day—an honest schedule that reflects the way our time has been spent for the past three or four days. Right off the bat, one will find that he spends a good deal of time on trivial things. The next step is to translate the budget into a weekly time budget—as many college and high-school students do.

A good budget is made up of the proper time allotments for sleep, recreation, study and—most important of all—quiet moments alone with the Bible, or in church, or in a Bible study class, and in searching for God and God's will in a meaningful way. Obtaining the good things in life—a sound body, a good job, good friends—is only one result of budgeting time. The most important part is obtaining faith in Christ, for everything else comes to an end if you haven't gained the promise of continuing life after death. Christ said, "I am the way, the truth, and the life: no man cometh unto the Father but by me" (John 14:3).

If I were to give a gift to everyone reading these words, I could choose from a number of things. I could offer you a good job. I could offer you money. I could offer you an important position, which would give you prestige. I could lead you into all sorts of opportunities and help you meet all sorts of influential

97

people. But these are not the gifts I would offer. These are temporary and passing—attractive for the moment, but destined to be destroyed in time.

No, the gift I would offer, if I were able, would be *time*—time for you to *find out who you are*. Time for you to sort out your life and discover the true values of life. I would give you a gift of time, and I would say: "Here is your time. Spend it and lose it. Or invest it and you'll live off the dividends forever." Whoever you are, wherever you are, whatever your lot in life, poor or rich, regardless of race, color, creed or ethnic background—time is in your hands to use as you will. What you *will* be depends upon how you use it. "Live life, then, with a due sense of responsibility, not as men who do not know the meaning and purpose of life but as those who do make the best use of your time, despite all the difficulties of these days" (Ephesians 5:15-16, PHILLIPS).

The most successful men I know are the busiest. It doesn't seem possible that they have time for anything, yet they seem to have time for *everything*. A lot of them helped to support their families, when they were in school, but they saved some time to invest in the future—to search for God and understand Him.

In the future, they are going to have all the time in the world.

During my years in business, I have met many businessmen who are successful; not all of them are happy, however, because they find their work boring. One such man I know, decided on a particular business field because it offered him the quickest road to wealth and prestige. Yet, when he was in college, his talents and interests lay in another direction entirely—toward a profession that would not have gained him very much money.

Today, this man is wealthy. He has a beautiful office, in a big city, and is respected in the community for his many responsibilities—but he is chained to his desk. He is a prisoner. Like King Midas, he has found that food that turns to gold cannot satisfy the appetite.

Another man I know was even more brilliant in school than

98

the first man. He showed tremendous promise, and it was expected that he would go directly into business after college and make a whopping big success of himself.

But this man knew something about himself. He knew that he would never be happy in business and that his real interests lay in education. So, he made a deliberate choice—one that he knew would cost him money in the long run. He took a job as a teacher in a small community. He rose to become the superintendent of schools in his area, which is the top of the ladder in his field. Although that man is not wealthy, he is doing the thing he loves best, with all the energy and talent he possesses. To him, there is no boredom, no routine; his work is a challenge and a delight. He is a genuinely happy man.

Anyone who is planning a career needs to ask himself some questions—for his own future happiness.

Among the questions should be these: *Does it make use of my talents? Am I interested in the work? Am I physically fit for it? What is the future for me in this work? Are my motives purely selfish, or will this give opportunity for me to serve my fellow man? Is my choice of this work part of God's plan for my life?*

To put it more simply: Realize that *you* are *you*, that whatever you choose to do in life eventually should be in accord with your own thoughts, interests and talents and in accordance with God's will for you. The work of a doctor, for example, would be the most painful drudgery for a man whose temperament, skills and personality would better fit him to be a first-rate airline pilot.

Many people today are locked into occupations that do not satisfy them at all, because they didn't take time to analyze intelligently what their true talents and interests were when they were younger, or because they sacrificed a chance to do work that they liked, for work that offered more immediate financial gain. It is a tragedy to look upon our work as a void that takes its toll of time and strength and gives nothing in return but wages!

99

An anonymous writer has said: "The beauty of work depends upon the way we meet it. Whether we arm ourselves each morning to attack it as an enemy that must be vanquished before night comes, or whether we open our eyes to the sunrise to welcome it as an approaching friend who will keep us delightful company all day, and also makes us feel at evening that the day was worth its fatigues." We don't know the name of the man who wrote those thoughts, but there are a host of men over thirty years old today who would immediately tell you that they wished they had read his words many years ago.

A great deal of family unhappiness results from situations where the man of the house is laboring at work he doesn't like to do. Certain talents have been given to each of us and they are ours to develop and protect. Both God and man will judge our success or failure, and about the worst mistake anyone can make is to deny his own interest and abilities to choose a career that will be meaningless to him, both spiritually and emotionally. Thoreau said: "The mass of men lead lives of quiet desperation." The challenge is not to be like most men, but to be *yourself!*

To develop your talents, a high-school education is absolutely indispensable, and it is available to all, even if you have to help support the family. Not every man will choose to go on to college, but there is much that can be learned through experience and practice. Still, college is better for most young people, and many of the most successful men in the United States today went through college the hard way: They earned it by waiting on tables, running errands, sweeping up dormitory halls.

For those who find everything difficult to do and have no apparent gifts, and to whom opportunity and improvement are limited, a careful analysis of themselves will reveal several things they *can* do well. In a small town in Michigan there was a boy who was singularly awkward and ungainly, and who found it difficult to compete in sports or to join his friends in their fun. He couldn't swing a baseball bat very well, but he had more than ordinary ability with a paintbrush. He applied himself, and before long he was earning a respectable living in the one thing he could do well and loved doing. That man is happier than many successful businessmen I know who *don't* like what they're doing. For example, I know a man—a writer—who became so involved in earning a living that he *envied* the young man who came to his estate to clean up the lawn. The young man actually saw more of the estate, and enjoyed it more, walking under the trees and eating his lunch by the pond, than the owner of the estate could ever do! I would like to be able to tell you that this same young man went on to become a landscape gardener or a tree surgeon, or at least chose some form of occupation in which he was outside and next to nature. Unhappily, he chose to go to work in a factory for the greater money it promised him in the beginning, and he regrets it to this day. Some men enjoy working in a factory, and it is honorable work, but this man didn't, so he didn't belong there. That's a sad ending to what might have been a happy story.

The Bible tells us: "Whatsoever thy hand findeth to do, do it with thy might . . ." (Ecclesiastes 9:10).

If Thomas Edison had given up in despair after his first failure, the progress of lighting would have been long delayed. If Louis Pasteur had sought something easier to work on after his many discouragements, the battle against disease would have been much farther from victory than it is now. The story of Abraham Lincoln—once called by his school teacher "one of the most dismal of students"—is a story of failure after failure, until he reached the White House and achieved undying success.

If a person keeps the right ideals and objectives before him, his chances of succeeding are greatly heightened. When we have determined what our true talents are, have dedicated them to a single worthwhile cause, have realized that they are a gift from God and not to be accepted lightly or without responsibility, we can overcome obstacles and adverse circumstances. Success won't come overnight. It takes patience and hard work, perhaps even bitter experiences that will test every bit of endurance we

101

have. But, if we have chosen wisely in the beginning—not been influenced by all the temptations to take "just any job" to get a car, or clothes, spending money for dates—we have approached the problem intelligently and will select work we can do well and that will give us happiness and strength to see it through to a successful conclusion.

No one has ever succeeded whose policy it was to see how little he could do and just "get by." For a while, perhaps, but there is no lasting inner satisfaction to be gained that way. A wealthy man, whose money has come easily and without much effort, often envies the hard-working farmer who is fulfilling his mission in life as the wage-earner for his family. The farmer sleeps better at night—and that is a truth that I believe will last as long as this earth.

Be true to yourself. God has given you certain talents. Do not deny Him, and yourself, by rushing blindly into a career you will dislike for the rest of your life.

When you know what God has given you, you will know what you can give the world, and you will know the paths to true happiness and contentment for both you and your family.

John D. Rockefeller was one of the wealthiest men who ever lived. He was constantly called upon to speak and to give his opinions on many matters. So, it is not without some interest to us to know that he made this strong, clear statement: *"How above all other possessions is the value of a friend in every department of life without any exception whatsoever!"*

Mr. Rockefeller literally lived the American dream and rose to become successful beyond the imaginations of most men. Yet, when he took stock of his possessions, you see what he placed in the forefront—a true friend.

In the Bible, it is written: "Two are better than one; because they have a good reward for their labor. For if they fall, the one will lift up his fellow; but woe to him that is alone when he falleth; for he hath not another to help him up" (Ecclesiastes 4:9-10).

Throughout the literature of the world, in every country, and under every government, true friendship is praised above all material gain; not just because it would appear to be the right thing to say, but because, in the hearts of men, there is a common understanding and appreciation of the very real need for good friends. It is a universal necessity for happiness and success.

Choosing friends, therefore, becomes a serious matter. And it is serious in more ways than one. Men have been known to fail in life because they have chosen their friends unwisely. All of us have heard the old saying: "We are known by the company we keep." There is a great deal of truth in this saying, because we have a tendency to borrow the ideals of our friends, and their ambitions, and, too often, their weaknesses.

By "choosing friends," I don't mean going out and selecting them as we might purchase an automobile or a toaster. But those with whom we associate and identify most closely should have standards and patterns that are similar to our own. If we have high standards and a good character, we will attract others who have the same ideals, and it is on this level that lifelong friends are found. The Bible asks: "Can two walk together except they be agreed?" (Amos 3:3). And friendship is, above all, walking together in good times and bad.

To make a true friend, you have to be one. Sincerity is essential. If we like people, we look for the good in them and we're kind in our criticism of their faults. We talk of common interests and find their problems absorbing and interesting. This is the sort of unselfish interest we expect from them, so we give it as well as receive it.

There are times when we might be called upon to defend a friend whose name and character are being assailed. On these occasions, the finest values of friendship are brought forth. Remember the words of Christ: "Greater love hath no man than this, that a man lay down his life for his friends" (John 15:13). Just talking about our friendship is meaningless. The only proof of friendship is in action. No labor is too hard, no sacrifice too great, no time too precious, when the welfare of a friend demands them.

Of course, one of the greatest assets of a true friendship is that it builds character. For example, friends often take special privileges. They may criticize each other, accept favors as a matter of course, and may accept—and even suffer for—each other's shortcomings without rancor. Such friendship requires tolerance, patience, humility and unselfishness—factors that build character.

Many of you are familiar with the person who welcomes everybody's company. He chooses friends as a bee chooses honey—a drop here, a taste there. Many people like this kind of person, but very few put their trust in him. He lacks real friends in a crisis. He has no one with whom he can share a problem, and others do not seek his help when they have problems. This kind of person can be said to have many acquaintances, but no friends, and this "hail fellow, well met" type of person is generally destined for a lonely future. Sacrificing true friendship with a few people for popularity with a lot of people is as poor a bargain as being unusually cool and aloof and going through life wthout any deep friendship.

Being deeply involved with many youth projects and organizations, I find that discussions invariably get around to the best way of handling a boy-girl relationship. The answer, which may surprise you, is to be a true friend. And I am going to be absolutely frank.

To be more than a friend is inviting trouble. A girl's psychology is different from a boy's. If an uncaring boy is selfish enough to take advantage of a girl's natural wishes to be compliant and goes "too far" with her, he is merely satisfying an urge of the moment, but she has lost a prized possession, which she can never recapture. That loss can ruin a girl's future, and I will tell you frankly that the young man who does such a thing bears the responsibility for it. He, himself, will eventually want to marry and, I assure you, he will want a decent girl who has saved herself for marriage. Yet, he will know that he has sent another girl out into the world who cannot offer this gift to any man. That is not an easy thing with which to live.

Straight talk on this subject is necessary, because many modern psychologists—and certainly tons of our present-day literature—crusade for the sexual freedom of young people. This kind of freedom only leads to complete bondage, a lifelong sense of guilt and the realization, as a man grows older, that he has made a fool of himself and of all of the values he has finally come to treasure—if it isn't too late for him by then.

As for the girl, it is obvious that if her association with a boy depends upon heavy petting, he is not thinking of her beyond the moment and she is giving up a precious inheritance to someone who does not deserve it at all.

Friendship—true, caring, unselfish friendship—that demands from us a sincere concern for the other person's welfare, boy or girl, is a Christian responsibility. "Bear ye one another's burdens and so fulfill the law of Christ" (Galatians 6:2).

Anyone on this planet who will practice that precept has taken a long firm step toward understanding God's plan for his life—and that is incontestably the greatest prize and source of happiness man can achieve.

12

Your Mind and Your Money

THE BIBLE tells us that we are not our own, but that we have been bought with a price—the death of the Lord Jesus Christ. This means that nothing we have can be withheld from the Lord. It has been my observation that one of the most difficult things for a man to give up is his will. God's desire for us is that we honor Him first. Yet to do this means giving up personal ambitions and desires—finding out what He wants us to do. When we have taken this step, there are no limitations on what God can accomplish through our lives.

During the latter half of the nineteenth century, commercial ship-owners dreamed of a quick, short route between the Atlantic and Pacific Oceans. The logical place to build such a waterway was at the narrowest portion of Latin America—what is now called Panama.

The French were the first to try to build a canal across the Isthmus of Panama. They tried for nine years (1880-1889) and then ceased operations. A second French company failed again in 1889. The job that needed to be done was a tremendous one. The canal, to be useful, had to be at least fifty miles long, between one hundred and three hundred feet wide, and not less than forty-one feet deep. In the 1880's, this was an immense construction problem, requiring new techniques in engineering, new kinds of equipment and great financial resources.

When the French efforts failed, attempts to build the canal came to a halt until 1904, when the Americans took a look at the project and decided it could, in fact, be done.

And they built it, opening the Panama Canal to traffic in 1914.

The odds against any kind of success in those days were overwhelming but the "I can do it" attitude of Americans who trudged through those swamps, combated malaria and, eventually, bulldogged the canal through to completion, made the "impossible" possible. This is not to say that France could not have done it, had she tried again, or that some other country couldn't have also built the canal. But, whoever built it, the primary necessity was people with vision and indomitable determination. That, alone, was the secret of the completion of the Panama Canal.

Accomplishment after accomplishment has been built upon the ruins of a less determined builder and, when we say to ourselves, "By God's help I can," the victory we seek is about half won. Whatever our natural abilities, unless we condition ourselves to work and win—particularly in our mental outlook—inevitably, we will accomplish less than we should.

The Bible says: "As [a man] thinketh in his heart, so is he." Therefore, of all our traits, we should take care to train and discipline the mind. Some men may have more intellect than others, but those who most often fail in life are those who simply do not use what intellect they have. With determination and perseverance, a man of limited intellect can sometimes accomplish what geniuses, with less drive, could never hope to accomplish. Thus, we have a second key to the proper use of the mind, one of the greatest of all the gifts God has given us—the source from which every good thing we want in life can be obtained. To let the mind wither and languish is to deny ourselves, foolishly, those good things we want.

Training and disciplining the mind to provide for our security and happiness in life is not too difficult a problem. In America, we are privileged to have education available to all who seek it. No country is so blessed with schools, colleges, universities, technical institutes, libraries and home study opportunities as we. In one manner or another, everyone can find time to *learn* and increase his knowledge and understanding. I know successful men who had to leave school early in life to support their parents or other members of the family, but they *made* time to continue their education through reading and correspondence courses. They knew what they had lost in having to leave school, and they were determined not to let their education stop just because they couldn't sit in an actual classroom. Consider the immense number of high school dropouts we have today—young people who can't wait to get out of school, not because they have to support a family, but because they just think learning is a bore and a waste of time. Judge for yourself the difference between them and the successful men I just spoke about.

School trains the mind in the grouping of ideas, in the development of thought and in the practical evaluation of problems. It is a threshold only—a place where the mind masters the fundamentals that help a person to put his mind to real and practical use, eventually. The tragedy of our time is that so many young people leave school, when all they've learned is a few of these fundamentals. They may never learn more, and life passes them by swiftly.

So, the first step in making your mind work for you is to train it in the fundamental art of thinking—that means school: *as much school as you can get.* When the time comes that you know what you want to do in life, plan your education to provide you with every bit of knowledge about your subject that is available. You'll want a degree, yes, but your real quest should be to achieve mastery over your field of study.

I have discovered that reading is a great teacher, and the things you choose to read should be interesting to you and pertinent to your future plans. If this is the case, then you will enjoy the time you spend reading, and you will retain what you learn.

108

It would be foolish to use precious time to read trivia, and a disciplined mind will pass by the volumes of trash on most newsstands and in bookstores; seek out reading material of merit and purpose. The right reading, at the right time, can provide facts and information and ideas that will remain with you for the rest of your life and serve you usefully and profitably on many future occasions.

As your mind begins to show the results of its training, your thoughts will begin to express themselves in actions—and here is where the world sees how successful your mind-training program has been. The mind has its own system of checks and balances, and these spell the difference between a weak character and a strong one. If you have a rash thought, the disciplined mind will call upon its accumulated knowledge and experience and convince you that your intended course of action is not wise. The man who has failed to train his mind beyond mere fundamentals has little or no ability to check himself, and he acts as rashly and foolishly as his first thought directs. His lack of judgement affects everything he does in life—his home life, his career, if he has one, his grasp of religion and the eternal values on which his happiness and future depend.

A wise man thinks of his mind as a tool—an important, finely-crafted tool that can be of inestimable value to him, if he takes care of it and uses it with care. This tool can enable the man to achieve almost anything, or it can destroy him, if it is not given use and is allowed to rust away.

Finally, and most important, a person with wholesome, disciplined thoughts stands on the threshold of understanding God's plan for his life—this, by far, is the most valuable service the mind can render. In the complicated world of today's adult, with pressures and philosophies attacking him from all quarters, fortunate are the men or women who can face the complexities and contradictions and see God's plan for them clearly.

This is the ultimate service of the mind and the thoughts of the heart.

"Thou wilt keep him in perfect peace whose mind is stayed on thee" (Isaiah 26:3).

The subject I am going to talk about now is money. We have already discussed time, talents, friends and the mind, and I've shared with you the many things I've come to understand and learned during the past seven decades. Money is the final subject, and I've saved it until last because the proper attitude toward money, and its proper use, are perhaps more misunderstood than any subject on earth. That is quite a statement, but I believe it it true.

Money is *trust*.

"The earth is the Lord's, and the fulness thereof; the world, and they that dwell therein" (Psalms 24). With these words, and with similar sentiments in other places in the Bible, God has made clear to all men that everything on this earth is God's and that we *own* nothing. Indeed, we *owe* it!

We are trustees, therefore, of every material thing we possess. We are obligated to use money for the things that last, rather than for things that perish. We are obligated to use money for the things that develop character, rather than for the things that destroy it. "And God is able to make all grace abound toward you; that ye, always having all sufficiency in all things, may abound to every good work" (II Corinthians 9:8). Think about that quote if you're ever tempted to doubt what money is for and are on the verge of spending it for a pin-up magazine, for example, which enriches the bank accounts of those who delight in corrupting this country's morals.

Now, let me give you some basic, hard-learned facts about money. First of all, no one can fully appreciate the value of a dollar until he has earned his own money. You've heard that a million times, and the reason you've heard it a million times is because it's true. The boy who has everything given to him is being deprived of one of the greatest opportunities for character building. It is a very wise father who, even though he could give

110

his son many things, convinces him that he should earn some of the things he needs.

There are many ways to illustrate this, but here is a true story about two cousins:

One of them was given a bicycle by his father, but the other boy earned his by selling magazines. The unearned bicycle was left out in the rain. It was neglected, ridden roughshod, and was soon fit for the junkheap. The other was oiled and kept in repair. Carefully used, it lasted a long time.

The difference in these bicycles resulted from the sense of values that had been instilled in the minds of the boys. One knew what the bike was worth, the other didn't.

A large proportion of the men who are leaders in American business are men who learned the value of money the hard way, early in life. This is a fact. There is therefore a strong relationship between successful businessmen and what should be the simple experience of every youngster—an opportunity to earn some of the things he needs.

When money is held, its real worth is absolute zero. Only when money is given out does it have any value—it takes more skill and practice to get rid of money profitably than it does to acquire it.

For example, one way to get rid of money is to buy something —let's say a suit. To get the most for your money—to get rid of your money profitably—you will have to ask yourself if buying the cheapest suit is the best course. Or, would it be better in the long run to buy a better-made, slightly more expensive suit? It is important to recognize values and to know an opportunity when you see one. Just the simple action of *thinking* about these factors before you buy, not reacting to the splashiest advertisement or fastest-talking salesman, can often result in true economy.

You will also get rid of your money more profitably, if you take a long look at finance plans before you jump into a purchase. In installment buying, often, the impression is given that an expensive item can be had for just a few dollars. But the burden of succeeding payments may well outlast the item. Some finance plans can increase the real cost of an item substantially, and it is a poor businessman who buys anything on "time," without first knowing and carefully considering what the final cost of the item will be.

Investments, of course, offer the greatest opportunity for getting rid of money profitably. There are many forms of investments. First, there are profitable investments to be made in worthy Christian projects, and the returns on these investments are in the joy of helping other people strengthen their faith in God. Then, there are investments in material things such as securities, savings plans that pay you interest, government bonds, etc. The key rule in all these types of investment opportunities is to know what your own investment goal is, and then get the sound advice of a trusted and competent professional.

Another aspect of money is debt. It is no disgrace to be in debt, but it is a disgrace to remain there. It is very easy to fall behind, but true character reveals itself in the refusal to stay there.

There are many blessings we receive in life which can not be measured in terms of money or material things. Let me give you an illustration of that type of blessing.

In January of 1954 I learned that I had been chosen to become President of Rotary International, for its great Golden Anniversary year of 1955. For twenty-five years before that Mrs. Taylor and I were teachers of the high-school group in our church. We had about sixty-five high-school students in the class. Mrs. Taylor taught the girls, and I taught the boys. I knew that the President of Rotary International and his wife would have to be away most of the time and out of the country a good deal. It was necessary for us to give up the Sunday-school class. We notified the Sunday-school superintendent and, at a meeting of the Board of the Sunday school, they chose our own daughter, Beverly, to take Mrs. Taylor's class, and our son-in-law Allen Mathis, Jr. to teach my class. Twenty years before that time, for a three-year period, Beverly and Allen were members of our Sunday-school class. Now, *there* is a blessing, which you just can not measure in material terms.

Many of the most valued things in life can not be measured in material terms. They are the unseen, intangible, eternal things that have to do with such eternal principles as the truth, justice and love of God and fellow man.

You'll sometimes hear it said that it's impossible for an honest man to be successful in business. Well, you've read about The Four-Way Test and you know that such a statement is untrue, and I'm happy to tell you that many American businesses are built entirely on the principle of honesty, dependability, and giving true value. Don't be misled by foolish remarks. More often than not, they echo the character of the man who makes them.

Until we understand that money is a blessing from God to make the lives of others happier, we have missed its true meaning and usefulness, and it is in the area of responsible "giving" that we fulfill our deepest obligation to God. The rich young ruler who came to Jesus, wanting to be His follower, could do everything that Jesus demanded—except give his money away to the poor. As a result, he left Jesus without getting the eternal joy and blessings which Jesus offered to him.

One duty of a Christian is to tithe his income. That is, set aside 10 percent of all his income—weekly, monthly or annually —to be used in the Lord's work. (Note I Corinthians 16:2: "Upon the first day of the week let every one of you lay by him in store, as God hath prospered him. . . .") This is basic to mature Christian growth and the minimum requirement. But I do not believe we truly begin to see what God can do with our lives until out of gratitude we give *more* than 10 percent. This becomes our "offering" to the Lord. From this point on, I believe that we begin to see the "returns" that come from devotion to our Lord. I also believe that a married couple should begin to tithe, immediately after they are married. It is my experience that the longer they wait, the more difficult it will be to start.

113

13

A True Christian
—a Good Citizen

THE GREAT SUCCESS of The Four-Way Test—by that I mean its demonstrated power to truly transform lives and provide the basic platform on which personal progress and happiness has been built for many people—has led me to search for clear and concise answers to several important questions. Foremost among the questions are these two: "What is a Christian?" and "What is a good citizen?"

Both questions are infinitely complicated, and the answers, which might apply in some cases, simply do not hit the mark in other circumstances. For example, there are nearly 300 differing denominations in the American religious community, all of them labeled "Christian." One denomination states flatly that a man is not a Christian unless he is a member of that particular denomination. Others hold that a man is not a Christian unless he obeys certain non-Biblical restrictive rules.

There are some who confuse the situation entirely and say that a Christian is anyone who is non-Jewish. This is ridiculous. There are many people of Jewish background and origin who have accepted Christ as Saviour, and are therefore Christians— the first of these were the Apostles!

Christ knew the chaos and imperfectness of this world, in which even the best of faithful men are sometimes at odds on important issues, as recorded, for example, in Acts 15:1-2, regarding the matter of circumcision. Indeed, one of the deepest meanings of Christ's sacrifice on the cross was to relieve men of the burden of sin and error and of the consequences of "seeing through a glass darkly." Differences among faithful men are bound to prevail until Christ's return.

So, in searching for a clear, well-defined and easy-to-understand statement of "What is a Christian?", I have given great consideration to the extreme complexity of the problem.

Christ himself answered the question simply: "Whosoever believeth in me shall never die, and though he be dead, yet shall he live" (John 11:25).

The Apostle Paul answered it in Romans 10:9: ". . . if thou shalt confess with thy mouth that Jesus is Lord, and shall believe in thine heart that God raised him from the dead, you shall be saved."

And there are many, many places in the Holy Scriptures where we see the love of God toward all those who accept His Son in faith and confidence. Such men are, truly and simply, Christians, by God's own Word.

Therefore, my concern is with the *visible* aspect of being a Christian—in other words, a simple yardstick by which we can generally distinguish a true Christian. It is not infallible—for few people would have distinguished the thief, who died on the cross next to Christ, as a Christian. But Christ promised him Paradise, and, indeed, that is the hope of all Christians.

After much prayer, I was led to write "Twelve Marks of a True Christian."

Each of the twelve marks is followed by two carefully and prayerfully selected Bible passages. You will find that the Bible passages confirm the content of the particular mark they follow.

TWELVE MARKS OF A TRUE CHRISTIAN

1. *He has accepted Jesus Christ as his personal Saviour and Lord.*

    But as many as received him, to them gave he power to

become the sons of God, even to them that believe on his name.

John 1:12

For God so loved the world, that he gave his only begotten Son, that whosoever believeth in him should not perish, but have everlasting life.

John 3:16

2. *He loves God with all his heart and expresses his love through constant prayer, praise and thanksgiving.*

And thou shalt love the Lord thy God with all thine heart, and with all thy soul, and all thy might. And these words, which I command thee this day, shall be in thine heart: And thou shalt teach them diligently unto thy children, and shalt talk of them when thou sittest in thine house, and when thou walkest by the way, and when thou liest down, and when thou risest up.

Deuteronomy 6:5-7

Be careful for nothing; but in every thing by prayer and supplication with thanksgiving let your requests be made known unto God. And the peace of God, which passeth all understanding, shall keep your hearts and minds through Jesus Christ.

Philippians 4:6-7

3. *He has a deep and abiding faith in the truth of God's Word and reads it regularly to strengthen his faith.*

. . . faith cometh by hearing, and hearing by the word of God.

Romans 10:17

Man shall not live by bread alone, but by every word that proceedeth out of the mouth of God.

Matthew 4:4

4. *He follows Christ's commandment, "Love one another"; he is quick to forgive others their trespasses against him.*

> A new commandment I give unto you, That ye love one another; as I have loved you, that ye also love one another.
>
> John 13:34

> Therefore if thine enemy hunger, feed him; if he thirst, give him drink; for in so doing thou shalt heap coals of fire on his head. Be not overcome of evil, but overcome evil with good.
>
> Romans 12:20-21

5. *He constantly seeks the guidance of the Holy Spirit as to God's will for him and follows God's commandments as to his thoughts, words and deeds.*

> Howbeit when he, the Spirit of truth, is come, he will guide you into all truth: for he shall not speak of himself; but whatsoever he shall hear, that shall he speak: and he will shew you things to come.
>
> John 16:13

> Not every one that saith unto me, Lord, Lord, shall enter into the kingdom of heaven; but he that doeth the will of my Father which is in heaven.
>
> Matthew 7:21

6. *He contributes of his income, as the Lord directs, to Christian projects and is an active and faithful member of his church.*

> . . . He which soweth sparingly shall reap also sparingly; and he which soweth bountifully shall reap also bountifully. Every man according as he purposeth in his heart, so let him give; not grudgingly or of necessity: for God loveth a cheerful giver.
>
> II Corinthians 9:6-7

> If any man serve me, let him follow me; and where I am,

there shall also my servant be; if any man serve me, him will my Father honour.

John 12:26

7. *He faithfully seeks to be more Christlike and is sincere, just, honest and dependable in his relations with others in home and community life.*

But speaking the truth in love, may grow up into him in all things, which is the head, even Christ.

Ephesians 4:15

Let your light so shine before men, that they may see your good works, and glorify your Father which is in heaven.

Matthew 5:16

8. *He knows that he is accountable to God for all of his possessions including his time, talents and property, and does his best to be a good trustee.*

So then every one of us shall give account of himself to God.

Romans 14:12

The earth is the Lord's, and the fulness thereof; the world, and they that dwell therein.

Psalm 24:1

9. *He is a humble person and gives God the credit and glory for his accomplishments.*

He hath shewed thee, O man, what is good: and what doth the Lord require of thee, but to do justly, and to love mercy, and to walk humbly with thy God.

Micah 6:8

Trust in the Lord with all thine heart; and lean not unto thine own understanding. In all thy ways acknowledge him, and he shall direct thy paths.

Proverbs 3:5-6

10. *He has a deep appreciation of what Christ did for him on the cross, readily witnesses for his risen Lord to others and expectantly waits for His return in person.*

> That if thou shalt confess with thy mouth the Lord Jesus, and shalt believe in thine heart that God hath raised him from the dead, thou shalt be saved. For with the heart man believeth unto righteousness; and with the mouth confession is made unto salvation.
>
> Romans 10:9-10

> And while they looked stedfastly toward heaven as he went up, behold, two men stood by them in white apparel: Which also said, Ye men of Galilee, why stand ye gazing up into heaven? this same Jesus, which is taken up from you into heaven, shall so come in like manner as ye have seen him go into heaven.
>
> Acts 1:10-11

11. *He is cheerful, patient, calm and trusts confidently in God to provide the means to overcome temptations.*

> But the fruit of the Spirit is love, joy, peace, longsuffering, gentleness, goodness, faith, Meekness, temperance: against such there is no law.
>
> Galatians 5:22-23

> There hath no temptation taken you but such as is common to man: but God is faithful, who will not suffer you to be tempted above that ye are able; but will with the temptation also make a way to escape, that ye may be able to bear it.
>
> I Corinthians 10:13

12. *He does his part, as the Lord directs, in carrying the gospel message of Christ to all peoples of the world.*

> And Jesus came and spake unto them, saying, All power is given unto me in heaven and in earth. Go ye therefore, and teach all nations, baptizing them in the name of the Father,

and of the Son, and of the Holy Ghost: Teaching them to observe all things whatsoever I have commanded you: and, lo, I am with you alway, even unto the end of the world.

Matthew 28:18-20

... Thus it is written, and thus it behoved Christ to suffer, and to rise from the dead the third day: And that repentance and remission of sins should be preached in his name among all nations, beginning at Jerusalem.

Luke 24:46-47

While I was serving as President of Rotary International I was led to believe that there should be written the marks of a good citizen, which might be accepted by the citizens of all of the free countries of the world. I talked with scores of leading business and professional men in many countries of the world before deciding on the final *Ten Marks of a Good Citizen.*

It is my opinion that nearly everybody wants to be a better citizen and contribute meaningfully to the society and government in which he lives, both locally and nationally, as his talents and interests lead him. Anyone who fulfills these *Ten Marks of a Good Citizen* is of great benefit, not only to his society, but to himself and to those dear to him. It is my hope and prayer that they will assist you in becoming a better citizen of your own community and country.

TEN MARKS OF A GOOD CITIZEN

1. *He is well-informed on local and world affairs.*

He takes the time to study local conditions and find out if his community is efficiently and effectively governed. He finds out how taxes are raised and expended. He judges the character and ability of local public officials . . . their ideals, training and experience . . . their *fitness* for public office. He knows what current public questions are and he asks himself how he can help to form sound public opinion.

He studies world conditions and learns as much as he can about his country's foreign policy.

2. *He is courteous, unselfish, friendly—gets along well with others —is a good neighbor.*

As good citizens, we should help our neighbors and fellow citizens in the development of their particular capabilities and personalities. Remember that the people you call "good neighbors" in your home community are those who are courteous, unselfish and friendly. They show that they like you by the way they treat you. They go out of their way to help make you happy and to assist you in time of trouble. We all want to be surrounded by good neighbors, so to have them we must also *be* a good neighbor.

3. *He is sincere, dependable, and takes an active part in the church or religious community of his choice.*

Truth and honesty are essential qualifications for real, last-ing success in life . . . and the character of a city or nation is the average of the ideals and character of all its citizens. We must always ask ourselves what we are doing to bring this average up or down.

If individual citizens suffer, or are poorly housed, or are undernourished spiritually, mentally or physically, there is bound to be an unhealthy reaction on the balance of the community. For the common good, therefore, we are indeed our brother's keepers, and this is a fact which no good citizen can ignore.

I once lived for a short time in a churchless community, and I do not want that experience again. As Benjamin Franklin said at America's Constitutional Convention: "God governs in the affairs of men." If a sparrow cannot fall to the ground without the Lord's notice, can an empire rise without His aid?

121

President Eisenhower said: "Faith is the mightiest force man has at his command. The true cure for the tensions that threaten to produce war lies not in guns or bombs, but in the spirit and minds of men." John Foster Dulles echoed the same thoughts when he said: "There is a moral or natural law not made by man which determines right and wrong, and conformity to this law is indispensable to human welfare. In human affairs, the non-material, spiritual element is more important than the material."

Therefore, it is essential for us to properly develop the moral and spiritual side of our lives—for our own sake and for the community's—and to be a good citizen we should take a part in the church or religious community of our choice.

4. *He appreciates what others have done for him and accepts responsibility for the future betterment of his community.*

We have others to thank for most of the blessings we enjoy today; the wonderful leaders of strong character who founded our country, the great spiritual and educational leaders who founded our churches and schools and colleges.

We should appreciate what our relatives have done for us, particularly our mothers and fathers. We also must thank the public officials in our home communities for their pioneer efforts and foresight in guiding the growth of our communities, and for public parks and beautiful trees along our streets. The elm trees around my home were planted by some lover of trees about 100 years ago.

A good citizen not only appreciates what others have done —and I have pointed up only a very few examples—he should also have a sincere and deep-seated desire to do things for others who are to follow him. He takes an active part in projects which will better his community.

Each one of us should be prepared to give a fair share of

our time, talents and money to help make our community a better place in which to live.

5. *He is fair and just in his relations with others.*

If we were all fair and just, there would be no need for courts and jails. To develop fairness and justice within himself, the good citizen constantly strives for the moral and spiritual values on which fairness and justice are based . . . and he practices them in his home, in his business and in his relationship with everyone he meets. Even if others are not fair and just with him, he remains true to his own values and the eventual result is to set an example that many others will follow.

6. *He obeys the laws of his community and nation.*

David J. Brewer, in his book, *American Citizenship,* says: "Picture the glory of this Republic if in each individual life, there were fully disclosed a respect for the law, desire for justice, regard for the rights of others, remembrance of the poor and afflicted, encouragement of education and the helping hand to everything that is true, beautiful and good."

The most commonly broken laws are traffic laws, and it is estimated that more than half of the more than 50,000 people killed on our streets and highways last year were killed by people breaking one or more traffic laws.

We should know the laws and we should do our best to obey them. If the laws are not just, we should use our influence to have the laws changed.

7. *He votes regularly and intelligently at election time.*

Justice Brandeis said: "The greatest menace to freedom is an inert people." It has also been said, "The price of liberty is eternal vigilance."

It is common in presidential elections in this country for

only about 60% of the eligible voters to go to the polls. A good citizen would never even think of not voting.

To vote intelligently, we need to know the character, ability and experience of the candidates; the parties; their policies; and we need to know the pro and con on public questions and how the parties and candidates stand on these questions. When it comes to voting, a good citizen makes sure he knows who and what he is voting for.

8. *He is interested in the freedom and welfare of all the world's peoples and does his part to secure them.*

To help people in other lands—and to understand their problems and act intelligently—we need to inform ourselves about their spiritual, physical and mental conditions. We can gather this information from many sources, and we can start by being kind, friendly and helpful to the many foreign students and visitors in our midst.

The good citizen does his share in subscribing to charitable and other programs which are destined to aid people in other lands. And he can pray for those in need behind the Iron Curtain whom he cannot otherwise contact.

9. *He is productive—renders a worthwhile service to his fellow man.*

The ne'er-do-well is not a good citizen. He takes from the community rather than contributes.

The good citizen uses his time and talent to produce quality—some article or service which is of real use to others. Some of us have different ideas as to what is a worthwhile service. Some would say that the liquor industry is not a worthwhile service, or that any form of gambling is not a worthwhile service. It is the character of the individual citizen that determines the answers to these questions.

10. *He sets a good example to the youth of his community.*

A good citizen realizes that he influences—for good and evil—everyone he contacts in his life, and this is particularly true when he contacts young people who are looking for ideals and values to copy in their own lives.

Elihu Root, former Secretary of State, said: "The success of all popular government lies with individual self-control (and example). This requires intelligence, so that the true relation of things may be perceived, and moral qualities which make possible patience, kindly consideration of others, a desire for justice, a sense of honorable obligation and capacity for loyalty to certain ideals."

Edgar A. Guest wrote a poem entitled, "Sermons We See." It is well worth remembering and goes like this:

> I'd rather see a sermon than hear one any day.
> I'd rather one would walk with me than merely tell the way.
> The eye's a better pupil, and more willing than the ear.
> Fine counsel is confusing, but example's always clear.
> The best of all the preachers are the men that live their creeds;
> For to see good put in action is what everybody needs.
> *(Used by permission—Reilly & Lee, Chicago, Ill.)*

By being good citizens—and setting the right examples—we will influence others to do the same.

A few years ago, a leading financial newspaper published the fact that the American Telephone and Telegraph Company had over six million dollars in losses during one particular year as a result of dishonesty by telephone users. (And I'm quite sure the figure has climbed since then.) The dishonesty included fake nickels, dimes and other contrivances applied to telephone pay-boxes, so the user wouldn't have to pay the telephone company for his call. At an average of 20 cents per call, that figures out to 30 *million times in one year* that Americans were dishonest enough to cheat the telephone company!

Using that story as a beginning—as an example of the widespread casual attitude toward simple morals and ethics—we can progress to juvenile delinquency, graft, corruption and the very real violence and crime which plague our nation so much that America has the dishonorable distinction of being the most crime-ridden nation in the world. Last year, Americans spent well over 10 billion dollars for alcoholic beverages, while our churches and foreign missions went begging for funds to support their absolutely vital work. The total budgets of all of our churches and their foreign mission projects last year were about six billion dollars.

History has proved again and again that freedom thrives and endures *only* where people live by God's rules. Truth, justice, love of one's neighbors, integrity—these virtues come from a strong religious faith, as do all the virtues of good citizenship. At the source of all that is good and decent and worth saving is the Creator of us all, and it is to everyone's benefit, personally and collectively, to acknowledge our nation's dependence upon God.

I have shown you that God had a plan for me. God also has a plan for you; He has a plan for your neighbor; He has a plan for the United States, and He has a plan for every country and person on this earth. No one escapes his scrutiny, and there can be little peace or satisfaction in a man's life until he conforms to God's wishes.

Twelve Marks of a True Christian and *Ten Marks of a Good Citizen* are simply guideposts—basic reminders of the qualities God wants to see in us *for our own good.*

Consider Communism for a moment—a violent, Godless faith, supported by treachery and deception, yet standing like a colossus over the minds and bodies of more than a third of the earth's peoples.

Why?

Because of the enthusiasm, sacrificial efforts and hard work of its followers.

Think, then, of what Christians could do! Supported by Almighty God, there could be a Christian awakening the likes of which this poor old world has never seen! A little over fifty years ago, about 150 men met in Moscow and launched Communism. If just 100 dedicated Christians met today, and each of them led just one person to Jesus Christ, by the end of this year, we would have 200 Christians. If each of these 200 Christians led one person to Christ by the end of the second year, we would have 400 Christians. Following this arithmetical progression, the entire world would be Christian in a lot less than the fifty years it took Communism to reach its present status!

Let us never forget that God reigns, and that we, of the free world, have access to the true faith, the eternal faith, the all-powerful and victorious faith evidenced in Jesus Christ and treasured by the founding fathers of our nation. *All things are possible with God*—in your own life and in the life of our country. I pray that each one of us does his part in seeking, understanding and following God's Word, for such a course is definitely the answer to our fears, our frustrations and the moral and ethical problems, which destroy the usefulness and progress of individuals and nations.

Let us all pray more, considering God before we act, speak and think, and let us all return to our Bible for the guidance and spiritual food that can change our lives in an instant!

If enough of us do this, I am certain that the dangerous clouds will pass away and we as a people—each one of us as an individual, regardless of our present state—will be blessed with peace, happiness and godly purpose.

I thank you for reading this book, and I pray that within these pages you have found the key to open the door on much more of that which is good and worthwhile for you and those who are dear to you.

God has a plan for you. Most of what our Heavenly Father wants done in His world must be done through us if it is to be accomplished in accordance with His will. Today our country and the countries of the world are faced with the following perilous conditions and problems. I am quite certain that God has a part for each one of us in His plans for the solution of these problems, so let us humbly ask Him where, when and how He can use us and then follow His will for us:

1. The problem of integration of the races in many countries around the world.
2. The problem of the rapid growth of the godless idealogy, Communism, and the slow growth of Christianity around the world.
3. The problem of the steady increase in crime and juvenile delinquency.
4. The problem of disrespect for and flaunting of the laws of most countries.
5. The problem of a great lowering of moral and ethical standards and practice.
6. The problem of increasing inflation and the lowering of the values of our money.
7. The problem of millions of poverty-stricken and starving people in a number of countries.

Now the God of peace, that brought again from the dead our Lord Jesus, that great shepherd of the sheep, through the blood of the everlasting covenant, make you perfect in every good work *to do his will*, working in you that which is wellpleasing in his sight, through Jesus Christ: to whom be glory for ever and ever. Amen (Hebrews 13-20,21).

An Update on Organizations Supported by Herbert J. Taylor

Child Evangelism Fellowship *(pp. 67-68)*
In 1982 Child Evangelism Fellowship reached almost 1.2 million children in the U.S.A. There are 7,500 Good News Clubs, and 290,000 children attended 5-Day Clubs. Their missionaries serve in over eighty countries.

Inter-Varsity Christian Fellowship *(p. 49)*
In 1982 Inter-Varsity Christian Fellowship had activities on 850 college campuses. The Nurses Christian Fellowship had 200 chapters. Over 165,000 college students have attended the triennial missionary convention in Urbana, Illinois.

Cedar Campus, frequently mentioned in this book, was acquired through the efforts of Herbert J. Taylor and now has the additional designation of The Herbert J. Taylor Center. The support of his Christian Workers Foundation has continued through the years, and as a result new facilities have been added including the Herbert J. Taylor Lodge and the Glory Forbrich Taylor Cabin.

Rotary International *(p. 71)*
In 1982 Rotary International had 911,000 professional men as members and more than 19,080 clubs in some 157 countries and geographical regions.

Young Life *(p. 64)*
In 1982 Young Life groups were active in almost 50 states and over 7,000 high-school teenagers attended various camps around the United States and Canada.

Basic Christianity by John R. W. Stott
Who on earth is Jesus Christ? What on earth did he do and why? What good resulted? John Stott examines the historical foundation of Christianity and explains the basics of the faith. His book is a good one to give to friends who are seeking and to help you reaffirm what Jesus Christ can mean to you. *142 pages, paper*

The God Who Is There by Francis Schaeffer
This first book by Francis Schaeffer contains the essence of his philosophy: historic Christianity, rightly understood and fearlessly applied, can solve the dilemmas of modern men and women. As he illustrates his ideas from modern philosophers, artists, writers and musicians, Schaeffer shows that he is both alive to our exciting world and sensitive to the despair that mars our achievements. *191 pages, paper*

Knowing God by J. I. Packer
This powerful book, now a classic, will draw you into intimate contact with the almighty God. As Packer discloses God's nature, you'll be filled with greater reverence and awe of the Living God and a more fervent desire to know him. *256 pages, cloth and paper*

The Fight by John White
You experience joy and triumph in your Christian life, but you know this joy doesn't come without struggle. In this very personal book, John White equips you to wrestle through the essentials: evangelism, faith, prayer, temptation, guidance, Bible study, fellowship and work. No matter where you are in your Christian walk, you'll find refreshing insights into the struggles and joys of freedom in Christ. *230 pages, paper*

Knowing God's Will by M. Blaine Smith
Smith explains how to find God's will, considering prayer, Scripture, reason, supernatural signs, desires, abilities, circumstances and the counsel of others. *141 pages, paper*

How to Understand Your Bible by T. Norton Sterrett
Afraid you just can't make sense out of the Bible but wish you could? Then this book is for you. T. Norton Sterrett presents general rules for reading the Bible's ordinary language and specific principles that apply to special types such as parables, figures of speech and prophecy. *180 pages, paper*